DECORATING KIDS' ROOMS

NURSERIES TO TEEN RETREATS

Better Homes and Gardens® Books
Des Moines, Iowa

Better Homes and Gardens® Books
An imprint of Meredith® Books

Decorating Kids' Rooms: Nurseries to Teen Retreats
Project Editor: Linda Hallam
Contributing Writers: Catherine Hamrick, Candace Ord Manroe,
        Sharon L. Novotne O'Keefe
Art Director: Jerry J. Rank
Copy Chief: Angela K. Renkoski
Copy Editor: Carol L. Boker
Proofreader: Jeanette Alt
Editorial Assistants: Susan McBroom, Karen Schirm, Barbara A. Suk
Art Assistant: Jennifer Norris
Production Director: Douglas M. Johnston
Production Manager: Pam Kvitne
Prepress Coordinator: Marjorie J. Schenkelberg

Meredith® Books
Editor in Chief: James D. Blume
Design Director: Matt Strelecki
Managing Editor: Gregory H. Kayko
Executive Shelter Editor: Denise L. Caringer
Vice President, General Manager: Jamie L. Martin

Better Homes and Gardens® Magazine
Editor in Chief: Jean LemMon
Executive Interior Design Editor: Sandra S. Soria

Meredith Publishing Group
President, Publishing Group: Christopher M. Little
Vice President and Publishing Director: John P. Loughlin

Meredith Corporation
Chairman of the Board: Jack D. Rehm
Chief Executive Officer: William T. Kerr
Chairman of the Executive Committee: E. T. Meredith

Cover photograph: Cheryl Dalton. The room is shown on *pages 42–43*.

All of us at Better Homes and Gardens® Books are dedicated to providing you with information and ideas you need to enhance your home. We welcome your comments and suggestions about this book on kids' rooms. Write to us at: Better Homes and Gardens Books, Shelter Department, LN-112, 1716 Locust St., Des Moines, IA 50309–3023.

DECORATING KIDS' ROOMS
CONTENTS

WITH A LITTLE THOUGHT and planning, you can create a happy room for your baby that will remain appealing into the elementary school years. The charm of a toddler's room starts in a simple way—with a lively striped fabric that's easy to live with. Choose a bright, unexpected color (here, peach coral) and pair with always-cheerful polka dots for long-term style.

ROOMS THAT GROW

CHILDHOOD
CHARM

MAKE A MURAL

Closet doors make the perfect canvas for introducing a mural into your child's room. An artist painted a country life scene, *page 6*, based on the colors of the fabrics and wallpapers. As alternatives, use stencils or wallpaper for your own creations or have your child hand-paint the walls with nontoxic paints. A toddler might just do his or her handprints; older children could paint family pets or

story characters. For easy application and cleanup, first paint the doors yourself with latex paint (a good-quality brush will give a smoother surface than a roller). For more on painting doors and some painting tips, see pages 100–101.

PAINT A SHELF

Special touches, such as a baby's treasures, make a room. Wall storage allows you to display the items safely out of reach, *below*. Construct a three-shelf unit from ¾-inch, paint-grade birch plywood. Prime wood and paint with blue and pink enamel for a smooth, durable finish. What makes this project fun are the rag dolls, traced from a pattern, cut from plywood with a jigsaw, and glued in place. To decorate, match artist acrylics to the colors of the room's fabrics. ■**TIP** If you can't find a pattern you like, use a motif from a children's book and enlarge the drawing (see page 103). Or, as a timesaver, look through precut decorative wood pieces at crafts stores.

MIX FABRIC AND PATTERN

Select your scheme-setting fabric first, then look for compatible coordinates in other patterns. Notice here how the complementary fabrics repeat at least one of the colors in the dominant fabrics and are the same intensity (brightness) of color. The lighthearted multi-polka dot printed fabric and the yellow-and-white plaid add different pattern types (print and plaid) but from the same color family.

Don't get hung up on exact color matches. Just look for shades of your colors that blend. ■**TIP** Don't be fooled by artificial store light. Ask for cuttings and take swatches home with you to try in your own natural or artificial light. Or, if you are shopping at an outlet miles from home, take cuttings outside to see how they blend in natural light.

S
SENS
smooth
corner bo
provides eas
accessible toy
young child; it ca
and teen treasures
shelves allow the co
wallpaper to show thro

Encourage neatness a
organization with safe, easy-
use storage. A three-tier,
three-section basket system,
top left, has slide-out storage
for toys and art supplies. Plastic
drawer dividers add extra
sorting options for crayons and
small toys. The desktop works
great for coloring and puzzles
now. Later, turn the unit into a
desk with handy storage on
either side of the knee space by
removing the center baskets.
(Use the extra baskets in a
closet for more organizing.)

JIZED
\ST A
\HOOD

ORAGE

\BLE SOLUTIONS With
\ed edges, a low, built-in
\okcase, above,
\y, safe, and
\ storage for a
\n hold books
\ later. Open
\rasting
\gh.
\d
\to-

...desk-
...rt into extra
...s as needed.

...you are remodeling or
...ding with an idea for future use,
plan for outlets. Think about where
the computer and/or telephone line
will go and make sure appropriate
outlets will be accessible. The color-
block scheme in this bedroom,
planned to take a 5-year-old through
the teen years, illustrates how.

• *The desk shelf is a standard 30
inches high.* For a comfortable
working height, the computer keyboard is on a lower shelf. A child-size
table and chairs offer other options
for games.

• *Built-ins with drawers below and
open shelving above* flank the desk,
which fits snugly under the window.
Though the top two bookshelves are

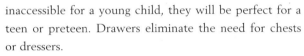

inaccessible for a young child, they will be perfect for a teen or preteen. Drawers eliminate the need for chests or dressers.

• *Storage needs grow with the child.* The twin platform beds, custom-built by a carpenter, eliminate the need for box springs. Pullout drawers, safer than toy boxes for little fingers, organize playthings. Later they will be perfect for extra bedding, sweaters, and sports equipment.

■**TIP** Mix drawer pulls for fun and organization. Different pulls and colored drawers help a young child know where to put clothes and toys.

BUDGET STRETCHER: Built-ins don't work for everyone. Beds with storage are available retail; check with stores that handle youth furniture. Or, simply be organized and colorful by painting an unfinished chest in this color-block style. (If it has wooden knobs, paint them in colors that contrast with the drawer fronts.) For touches of vibrant color, incorporate bright bumper pads for a baby and bed linens and simple window treatments for a child. Buy or sew large, bright floor pillows. Hang bold, matted, simply framed posters.

ABOVE: *Take advantage of the space under your child's bed for extra storage. If you plan to store heavy toys, ask your carpenter to build drawers from ½-inch plywood. For reinforcement, request heavy-duty drawer rollers and metal corner clips.*

LEFT: *Color—and lots of it—creates this stimulating scheme. Find a vibrant fabric and pull out three to six colors. When you are ready to redecorate, no problem. Choose a new scheme and get out the paint color charts. With proper base coats, even the most intense walls can go as pale as you please.*

CREATIVITY

STIMULATING COLOR. Given their druthers, kids gravitate to the floor for art and play.

Here's a fun finish to try: Paint the floor with chalkboard-type paint; allow it to dry and doodle designs with acrylic paints from the crafts store. Brush-tipped paint pens work well for doodling, too. The chalkboard paint is fun for walls, but seal it for floors with polyurethane. Polyurethane will make it easier to mop clean and wipe up any spilled paints. Tracked chalk dust is too high a price to pay for creativity. For more on chalkboard paint, see page 99.

Bright is an understatement for children's color choices. That is as it should be, according to recent studies in child development. Because bright, bold, primary colors and defined shapes stimulate learning, just a few touches will do the trick. If you prefer pale or white walls and ceilings, add a colorful mobile above the crib and swap it with another mobile from time to time.

ORGANIZED PLAY NOW HOMEWORK LATER

Your child may be years away from studying geometry, but you can apply the principles of divided, open spaces to organize his or her playroom. The secret to keeping toys and school gear neat and organized isn't just having enough space. It's having accessible storage your child will actually use. Here's how to organize a playroom that will grow with your child.

• *Locate a playroom where your child will be close to you, such as near the kitchen or family room.* Neither you nor your toddler will be comfortable with a playroom in the basement if you spend most of your time in the kitchen.

• *Measure what you will be storing before you start designing and installing shelves.* Think adjustable sizes rather than standard symmetrical arrangements. (Measure some bigger toys to make sure the shelves are adequately sized.) Avoid sharp angles and corners that can hurt a child.

• *Consider weight loads.* Most toys are fairly light, but a row of books can get heavy. Architects often specify ¾-inch-thick birch plywood for bookshelves; spans shouldn't be longer than 30 to 36 inches between supports. If you are using a thinner plywood, such as ½-inch, reinforce with supports every 24 inches.

PAGE 10: *Now toys and the child's art add the color, but this room will work equally well as a study area when books and sports equipment fill the shelves. A bulletin board or corkboard will fit the wall space above the adjustable desk. Treated to be stain-resistant, the rug adds color to the tightly woven commercial carpet.*

• *Think long-term storage needs.* Children's playrooms and bedrooms tend to be small, so take advantage of every bit of space by building shelving to the ceiling. Store what your child plays with every day on the lower shelves; rotate other toys and games to the top shelves.

• *Look at your material alternatives.* Economical painted particleboard, rather than laminate or birch plywood, works fine for built-ins.

• *Use labeled plastic bins, boxes, or baskets for small toys, such as blocks, cars, and plastic figures.* For young children, label with a picture of what goes in the bin.

• *Include an adjustable, lighted work surface.* With vertical shelf supports and L-brackets, a work surface can be raised as a child grows—the same way bookshelves are moved.

ABOVE: *Any wall works as an art center with this easy-to-execute idea. Hang a large roll of art or brown kraft paper from a wooden drapery rod and heavy-duty brackets. Encourage your child to leave work in progress in place for you both to admire. Working together is fun, too.*

PIECES WITH A PAST

If you love antiques and vintage-style decorating, share these interests in a child's room based on traditional furnishings. An armoire, cupboard, wardrobe, or small linen press is an ideal place to start—both for storage and as a focal point. Generally, smaller American, English, or European country pieces work better than larger, formal pieces in a child's room. Pine pieces can be good choices because they tend to be light and informal. Alternatives include new reproduction armoires or unfinished ones you stain, paint, or stencil yourself. **BUDGET STRETCHER:** Like the look of antiques without the price tag? Look for English or American reproduction furniture made in the 1920s and 1930s or new pine pieces crafted from old pine.

TIMELY DECORATING TIPS

• *Shop garage sales, flea markets, and secondhand stores for old toys and child-size furniture.* Because of concerns about old paint, brush and scrub items to remove any loose or chipping pieces. To be on the safe side, use old painted toys, even ones in good condition, only for decoration until your child is out of the gnawing stage. Look for old fabrics for pillows and cushions or incorporate some of the new faded-look fabrics for this vintage effect.

• *Sturdy 19th-century beds that survived pioneer treks are ideal for late-20th-century children, too.* Unlike many modern beds, they are built of solid wood. Pairs of beds are hard to find. If space is tight, settle for one. Or, mix two similar

but unmatched beds—for example, two cherry beds, but not a cherry and an iron bed. Bed linens tie the scheme together. Chairs need to be durable and comfortable. An armchair or rocker can be ideal to snuggle in when you and your child read together.

• *The old-toy look is fun, but a child's room isn't a museum.* Choose toys he or she can play with. A few untouchables are fine—such as these airplanes suspended from fishing line attached to the ceiling—but keep them to a minimum.

■**TIP** Help children decide on something they would like to collect so antiquing can be shared family fun. Depending on a child's age, you'll probably want to start with unbreakables such as unpainted wooden toys.

PAGE 12: *Build around a rugged daybed and wicker rocker for your son's first big-boy room; this look can last through the teen years. Classic sporting motifs are just as timeless.*

ABOVE: *Start with a classic floral rug and aged pine, and your daughter's room will grow up with charm and style. New or vintage dresses and pretty straw hats on a rack add quick-change, youthful accents. Muted pastels complete the look.*

ABOVE: *Furniture can last from tots to teens if you buy classic pieces, such as this painted dresser (easily topped later by a mirror), upholstered armchairs, bamboo table, and simple table lamps. Later such ageless pieces can work equally well in a sunroom or guest room.* **TIP** *Avoid juvenile theme lamps; they date quickly.*

RIGHT: *Don't have this much space for a large armoire? Use a narrower wardrobe or simple cupboard. Such a focal point will set your decorating mood, whether it's the French style shown here or American country. As an alternative, paint a plain, unfinished armoire and stencil on details.*

STYLISH STORAGE NOW & LATER

Do you like the idea of decorating a room that will follow your baby girl into her teens? You can purchase wallpaper, window treatment fabrics, an area rug, and even storage pieces only once. And you can re-cover an inherited chair in a fabric you and your child will enjoy for years.

AN EASY APPROACH

• *Choose a wallpaper that's feminine but not babyish.* The flower garden mural on this page adds a soft background for a pair of cribs but would be equally pretty for painted twin beds or upholstered daybeds. A hand-painted mural in another garden or floral motif provides another option. Or, you may prefer more abstract backgrounds as stripes or stars.

• *Shop for pretty fabrics in pastels, florals, or tiny prints.* Some of the novelty print fabrics based on tea cups or porcelain figures could be other choices.

• *For a boy, choose a plain painted background* and use a wallpaper border for color. Or, stencil a border that can be painted over. (It's doubtful you'll find a boyish theme a teenage boy will live with.)

• *A fairly tailored window treatment combined with sheers is a safe choice.* Louvered or plantation shutters are permanent window treatments that provide light and sun control. Look for durable upholstery fabrics in small prints or solid fabrics.

• *Acquire storage pieces that can be used through the teen years, then placed in other rooms or settings.* A dresser and armoire that are ideal for baby clothes and diapers will work equally well for jeans and sweaters.

VERSATILE PAINTED PIECES

For an inviting room now and for years to come, invest your time in painted furniture. Paint is the quickest way to bring

order and style to a mishmash of assorted woods and finishes. New cribs will take on the look of prized antiques when their soft white is decorated with hand-painted roses and bows. (For more on painting and stenciling furniture, see pages 43 and 106–107.)

• *To add much-needed storage,* paint an unfinished or thrift store chest or dresser to match. For extra detailing, hand-paint or stencil the top and cover it with protective, rounded-corner glass.

• *Add a side table* or a chair and you'll have a well-furnished room your daughter can grow up in gracefully.

A GIRL? A BOY?
FABRIC FUN FOR BOTH

Here's a nursery that's charming for either a girl or a boy—and with a cheerful, theme-setting fabric that will be fun for years to come. Best of all, the new heirloom-quality crib is designed to convert into both a budget-stretching youth bed and a double bed.

IDEAS FOR INSPIRATION

• *Look for coordinating wallpaper borders and fabrics* like those used in this carousel-themed nursery. Although this carousel animal fabric is youthful, it isn't babyish—a plus when you think long term.

• *Avoid fabrics and borders that are dominated by pastel blues or pinks.* But don't worry about using fabric with accents of either. The blue-and-yellow plaid fabric is a tailored neutral that works for a child or an adult.

• *Pick out the wall color from the fabric you select.* The yellow chosen for this room is a happy, easy-to-live-with traditional choice.

• *Hire an art student.* If you don't want to paint or stencil your nursery yourself, consider the budget stretcher of commissioning an art student or instructor to paint your motif. For this nursery, the fabric's carousel figures inspired a college student's creativity. Talented art students and teachers at your local college, junior college, or high school are all possibilities.

CRIB CONVERSION

You may be planning for the baby to sleep in an inherited family crib. But even if the bed meets current safety standards, its useful time is limited. As an alternative, this convertible mahogany-finish bed is designed in the style of a traditional 19th-century crib. (A new mattress will be required for full size.) More contemporary styles of convertible cribs are also available.

ABOVE: *It's fine to use a youthful print such as this carousel motif if the theme lasts beyond the crib stage.* **TIP** *Use a novelty print only for the valance; substitute a checkered fabric for side panels, shown for curtains.*

RIGHT: *Line and interline a canopy for long-lasting shape and style. For ideas on making your own, see pages 29 and 31.*

SWEET DREAM NURSERIES

WHETHER YOU'RE DREAMING OF PETAL pinks, baby blues, or primary colors when you're getting ready for baby, you're dreaming happy dreams. No room is more fun to decorate than the nursery, because no one is more special than your own little angel. The following pages illustrate project-filled nurseries for a variety of decorating tastes. So no matter if you're waiting for a girl or boy or planning to be surprised, there's a nursery just right for your wee one.

PINK &SWEET

For the old-fashioned girl, start with an antique iron crib, *page 19*, and Grandmother's hand-me-down wood furniture. Use old furniture with classic shapes, then add heirloom accents such as the focal-point quilt mounted on the wall. Pretty and appealing as it is now, the space provides room to grow: Only the crib needs replacing with a second twin bed as your little girl grows up. To remember this nursery as it was during baby days, her dad crafted a miniature version, complete with crib. It is preserved in an acrylic plastic box framed in wood and mounted to the wall as an artful accessory.

The keys to this nursery design lasting well into girlhood are age-neutral pinks, floral prints (no babyish motifs), and old furnishings refinished for a feminine look. To refinish your lucky finds or family treasures:

• **Strip old paint** from vintage pieces, then paint them crisp white. (Don't use stripper yourself if you are pregnant.)

• **Sponge pink paint over the white.**

• **Paint pale blue trim** along the furniture's moldings as outlined details. Seal with a clear coat of acrylic varnish.

• **Add new knobs and pulls** for an updated look that doesn't compromise the furniture's family connection or classic, fluid lines. (For more on painting furniture, see page 43.)

ABOVE: *Dad made a scale model of the nursery. As an easier alternative, paint miniature dollhouse furniture to match yours and display in a shadow box from a frame store.*
PAGE 20: *Use what you love to decorate your nursery. This family quilt, displayed above the twin bed, adds a wall of color. To avoid fading and damage, make sure your quilt isn't exposed to hours of direct sunlight every day. An odd dining chair, gleaned from a thrift store, sports new white paint and hand-painted details.*
TIP *If you prefer, stencil your details (see pages 106–107). To re-cover the seat, carefully pry it loose (check the underside, too) and wrap in a fabric scrap before replacing.*

BABY-PROOF

USING ANTIQUE CRIBS. The elegant antique iron crib on *page 19* provides a feast for the eyes, but it could have been dangerous without some adaptations for safety.

• **The crib's original vertical side bars were spaced too wide apart for infant safety. To ensure against the baby trapping her head between the bars, a metalworker outfitted the crib with extra bars. It now meets modern standards, with slats no more than 2⅜ inches apart.**

• **Before consumer safety laws, crib canopies weren't under scrutiny. But new knowledge of potential safety hazards means this crib canopy is best left bare, with no gauzy fabric that could possibly fall down and suffocate the infant.**

• **Placement of the crib keeps safety in mind, too. A window position would have provided more efficient use of space, but not without risking injury to an infant. Placing the crib away from the window prevents falls against the window or tampering with window blinds, curtains, and cords. (For more on crib and nursery safety, see page 27.)**

• **Stripping metal is difficult and time-consuming. You may want to have an old metal bed professionally stripped and primed. Paint with an enamel paint formulated for iron.**

LITTLE BOY BLUE

Cloud motifs add a soft, soothing background for a baby's or young child's room. If you like the look, here's one way to re-create it:

• *Paint walls with a white flat latex base.* Use a creamy off-white rather than a stark shade.

• *Apply sky blue glaze* with a small sponge roller in 3×3-foot sections. (Be sure you ask for glaze for decorative wall painting at the paint, hardware, or arts-and-crafts supply store.) Glaze adds depth lacking in standard paint.

• *Wipe away the blue glaze* with clean cotton rags (cotton T-shirts work well) to expose areas of white wall in irregular cloud shapes.

• *Soften the edges* with a 3- or 4-inch soft china bristle brush from an art store.

• *Stipple on a bit more blue glaze* with a soft 2-inch stippling brush to add even more contour to the clouds. (For more on stippling, including how-to techniques, see page 107; for another cloud painting technique, see page 103; for more decorative painting instructions and tips, see pages 104–105.)

For the other hand-painted features, draw them onto the wall with pencil (to avoid smudges, don't use the eraser); paint with acrylic paints. The ribbons are easy to start with.

PAINTING ALTERNATIVE
Instead of painting, make your own decals for walls or furniture. Purchase copyright-free clip art in your chosen motifs from an art supply store. Have motifs photocopied on heavyweight, cold-pressed art paper at an office services store.

Color the designs with watercolors, thinned acrylics, or colored pencils. Lightly wash with a soft-bristle paintbrush. Allow to dry, cut out with a sharp crafts knife, and glue to wall or furniture with water-based glue. For durability, seal furniture pieces with three or four coats of matte polyurethane.

ABOVE: *When space is tight and storage minimal, center the crib on a wall and add storage units on either side for a built-in look. Sew or purchase a window valance and hang above the crib—safely out of baby's reach.*

PAGE 22: *You can borrow from the closet by removing sliding doors as shown here. Substitute a painted baker's rack that will later work equally well in a breakfast room.*

INDIVIDUALITY

PAINT YOUR OWN LINENS. The nontoxic, water-based crafts paint that produced the picture-perfect hand-painted linens on this crib is designed for safe home use. To create your own painted linens, you'll need:

100-percent unglazed cotton fabric in white or pastels

Tracing paper; pencil

Waxed paper

Nontoxic water-based crafts paints in your choice of colors

Waterproof paint pens; fine short-haired brushes

Textile medium (available from crafts stores)

1 Wash and dry the cotton fabric to remove the sizing; otherwise, paint won't be absorbed.

2 Draw or trace your design on paper with a pencil first. Practice painting it to perfect your color combinations. The simpler the design, the easier the project.

3 Draw or trace your design onto tracing paper (available from an art supply or fabric store).

4 Tape the tracing paper to a light-filled window and position the fabric over the paper where you want the design. Trace onto the fabric with a soft pencil.

5 Cover a table with waxed paper and lay out the fabric. Outline the design with waterproof paint pens in your colors or with your undiluted paint and fine short-haired brushes. Fill in design with a half-and-half mix of water-based crafts paint and textile medium.

6 Allow to air-dry for 24 hours before cutting and sewing.

7 To clean, hand-wash in cool water with mild detergent.

SHIPSHAPE

More than patriotic, a salute to red, white, and blue creates a fun and doable theme that never looks dated. With anchors-aweigh wallpaper and childworthy nautical accessories, the room projects an ideal seafaring scheme. Add yellow accents and the primary palette is complete.

The three primary hues—red, yellow, and blue—are the building blocks for all other colors. Primary colors are strong enough to provide the visual stimulation a developing young mind needs. And best of all, they age gracefully, appealing throughout childhood. *Just one warning:* Even for tots, be sure to include plenty of neutral white as a soothing relief from the primary palette's powerful punch.

GETTING STARTED

• *Declare the nautical theme wall to wall* with tiny-print, anchor-studded paper. This wallpaper's white background keeps the primary colors in check as accents instead of too-bold main attractions.

• *Top the main wallpaper* with a more colorful sailing ship border in a larger scale to ensure there's no missing this room's motif. Striped paper below the chair rail increases the cheer. (For wallpaper how-tos and techniques, see pages 108–111.)

• *Limit furnishings to a few essentials* for the uncluttered look important to a nursery. A hard-working, multipurpose crib-chest is the primary space maker. All that's needed is a changing table to save an adult's back strain when dressing and diapering the baby and, of course, a rocking chair for starting off bedtime with sweet dreams.

• *Select furniture finishes* that blend with the rest of the room's palette. What could be softer than white wood and wicker for melting into the background?

ABOVE: *Display clothing and decorations such as nautical pennants to give your nursery personal style.*
PAGE 24: *Medium-weight cotton or a cotton-blend fabric gives necessary body and shape to the seagoing window treatment.*

SAIL AWAY

NAUTICAL TREATMENT.

Plywood cornice board cut to fit window; kraft paper

Batting

Staple gun

54-inch-wide medium-weight fabric (5 yards yellow, 4 yards red, 2 yards blue). *Fabric amount depends on size of window; this is for standard double-hung window.*

Matching sewing thread

Narrow ribbon; piping (optional)

Pair of L-brackets; 2 cup hooks

1 For accurate measurements, cut a curtain and cornice from kraft paper to use as patterns.

2 For cornice, wrap batting tightly around cornice board; staple. Measure fabric to cover cornice, including three pleats. Add seam allowances to sides.

3 Cut blue and yellow canvas to fit. Sew panels together, right sides facing. Leave opening. Turn to right side; press; sew closed.

4 Place center of panel at center of the cornice board. Mark pleats, hand-tack in place. Glue, staple, or tack panels to cornice.

5 For drapery, cut two red panels and two yellow panels (length is from top of cornice to floor; width is width of window). Sew each red panel to a yellow panel, right sides together. If desired, sew on piping. Leave opening. Turn; press; sew closed.

6 Make a buttonhole at lower inside corner of each panel.

7 Staple panels to back side of cornice board; overlap at top. Hang cornice from L-brackets. Bring inside corners to outside edge; screw cup hooks to wall. Slip narrow ribbon through buttonholes and tie to hooks.

RED, WHITE, & BRIGHT

If you're reluctant to make a color commitment in the nursery for fear of it being outgrown by your fast-growing child, relax. A two-color palette is easy to implement and easy to change, and it offers big returns for a small investment. A bright and bold color scheme can be created even within four white walls, provided a robust second hue such as red punctuates the rest of the room.

With the walls left colorless for a neutral background, it's up to other decorating elements—curtains, crib linens, chair cushions, or area rug—to go red. The upbeat red-and-white stripes and checks in this nursery support the theme from the Babar the Elephant children's books.

As the baby matures, changing the room's palette and theme is as simple as swapping these color-defining elements for ones in the newly chosen palette. No wallpaper to remove or new paint to apply reduces the work in redecorating, providing more energy for stimulating cosmetic changes that keep pace with your child's development.

OTHER DYNAMIC DUOS

White plus any other color offers the most versatility of a two-color scheme, but other combinations are also worth considering. Classic pairs such as blue and yellow, or the newer twosome of blue and green, make a good nursery palette, not too feminine or masculine. When it's time to change the room, one color can remain and be joined with a new partner for a fresh look.

RIGHT: *As versatile as it is fun, this nursery illustrates quick-change decorating. Just change the curtains and rocker cushion for a new color look.*
BELOW: *With a clean, bright white backdrop, your child's storybooks, stuffed animals and bright toys give style and personality to the nursery.*

CRIB SAFETY

The good news in crib safety is that all new cribs sold in this country must meet Consumer Product Safety Commission standards. The bad news is that antique cribs—some of the most appealing to nostalgic parents—are a gamble. To ensure your baby's safety, make sure any crib that you buy meets the following guidelines.

• Crib slats should be close together—no more than $2\frac{3}{8}$ inches apart—to prevent your baby's head from getting trapped.

• Drop-side catches that won't accidentally release prevent your baby from rolling out of the crib. A two-stage catch is best. An older-style crib with stationary upright sides is also acceptable for safety (if not for the parents' convenience).

• A snug-fitting mattress that doesn't allow room for more than two fingers between the mattress and crib prevents a child's head, arms, or legs from getting caught. Standard crib mattresses are $27\frac{1}{2}\times51\frac{7}{8}$ inches, but measure both crib and mattress to be safe.

• Also check any vintage or secondhand crib to be sure it doesn't have lead paint, cracks, shaky construction, loose hardware, missing slats, removable finials, or decorative knobs. Even if you're recycling a crib purchased new for your own older child, check for safety. The plastic strip covering the top rail can become brittle and crack over time, which is especially dangerous to an infant's eyes.

PRETTY, PRACTICAL, PEACH

Careful planning means your daughter's pretty nursery can be a smart long-term investment, too. When you choose fabric, furnishings, and colors with staying power, the room's background remains in place. For this classic decorating, the answer's not in animal or toy motifs but in a pastel palette (here, peach with rosy accents) and in classic fabrics that won't grow out of date as your child grows up.

Plaids, checks, and florals bespeak storybook pleasures even grown-ups love. They come together in furnishings that promise to stick around awhile: a classic club chair and ottoman dressed in matching ruffled skirts, frothy balloon shades, a floral needlepoint rug, and an array of printed throw pillows. Even the ruffled canopy mounted on the wall alongside the crib can stay, serving as a headboard fit for a princess when the baby moves into a standard twin bed or daybed.

PAGE 28: *The furnishings in this nursery will work for years to come. The chair and ottoman are comfortable now for snuggling and later can be a teen reading retreat. The crib's dust ruffle could become pillow shams or be modified into a twin bed skirt.*
RIGHT: *When space is tight, use a small corner cupboard for extra storage that won't be outgrown.*

SEW YOU CAN

SEW A CANOPY.

Plywood; wood glue

Paper, thread, pins

2 pairs of L-brackets

Fabric to size (see below)

Equal yardage lining fabric

Piping; pearl cotton

1 Use two layers of plywood glued together for a circular form. To make the pattern, draw a 24×33-inch oval on paper. Cut in half, leaving a 24×16½-inch shape. Fit flat side to wall, 7½ inches from ceiling, support with L-brackets.

2 Cut and piece fabric to make two panels, each ceiling to floor in length and 50 inches wide. Taper so center hangs 12 inches off floor and outer edge touches floor. Cut lining pieces to match. Finish inner edges with 3-inch ruffle and piping. Sew lining to curtain, right sides together; leave opening. Turn; press; sew closed. Gather edges around form; tack.

3 For valance, cut and piece panel 25 inches deep and 6 yards wide. Finish lower and short ends with ruffle and piping, curving shape at corners. Turn upper edge 3 inches for ruffle; stitch.

4 Starting at base of top ruffle, mark 15 to 20 rows for smocking; space rows ½ inch apart. Lay piece of pearl cotton along marked line; pin. Leave 6-inch tail at each end. Using wide zigzag stitch, sew over pearl cotton. Don't catch in stitch. Repeat for rows.

5 Starting at one end, pull all pearl cotton ends; gather to center of panel. Start at other end; gather remainder of panel. Pull gathers to fit form; overlap ends. Anchor pearl cotton with machine stitches. Staple valance to form. Adjust gathers to cover staples. Hang form on wall.

6 Sew two lined fabric bows. Pull curtains back with bows. Tie to wall-mounted hooks.

NOT-SO-PLAIN VANILLA

The mission for this nursery was to be stimulating but gender-neutral. What else can be done, after all, when the parents don't know—or don't want to know—whether the baby on the way is a boy or girl?

But neutral doesn't mean bland. There's nothing Melba toast-like about this small space. The innovative concept that brings it to sparkling life begins by first drawing a blank—that is, painting walls white as a blank piece of paper. The next steps are as easy as ABC.

• **Choose primary colors you want.** Purchase acrylic paints from the crafts store in your colors and several sizes of artist's brushes or small trim paintbrushes. For the look of brushstrokes, don't use foam brushes. **■TIP** Some people find it easier to work with wide-tipped or brush-tipped paint pens; do not use permanent or oil-based markers.

• **Draw your designs in the style** of a child's early artwork. The simpler the motifs the better. The parents-to-be drew the motifs shown here freehand for a spontaneous look. But if it makes you more comfortable, draw in soft pencil first. Or, use stencils for alphabet, numbers, and simple animals.

• **Pencil in the border.** Measure and use pencil dots and ruled lines for a rough placement of the border, then paint on the color freehand. (For more details on hand-painted walls, see pages 40–43.)

• **Add more color with fabrics.** Here, a vivid canopy in a bold array of gender-neutral hues attaches to the wall behind the crib. Beneath it, a fun but timeless lattice-work patterned area rug grounds the room in warm, cozy comfort, while still exposing some of the older home's original hardwood floor.

PAGE 30: *In this cheerful nursery, the naive charm of children's art takes center stage. Use small trim brushes for a hand-painted look.*
LEFT: *To add to the fun, paint stripes on an old rocking chair in the same bright motif.*
BELOW: *When you shop for a changing table, make sure it has safety guardrails on all four sides. Shelves underneath offer convenient, accessible storage.*

BIG TOPPER

CIRCUS TENT CANOPY. The one essential in any nursery is a crib, so why not make the most of that with a focal-point canopy? You'll need:

54-inch-wide fabric (see below for calculating yardage)

2 extra yards for binding

Backing and low-loft quilt batting in the yardage of your fabric (minus the 2 yards)

Thread and pins

2 narrow metal curtain rods; 4 cup hooks

Small stuffed animals

1 To determine the length of 54-inch-wide fabric you'll need, measure from the top of the baseboard to the ceiling. Add 60 inches for the canopy. Allow the same amount for the backing and batting and 2 additional yards for the binding. (Based on a 54×30-inch crib.)

2 Sandwich low-loft quilt batting between two layers of fabric, right sides facing out. Baste the layers together with pins or with loose basting stitches. Sew through all three layers at 3-inch intervals or along design lines.

3 Cut one end to the pointed shapes shown on *page 30*. Bind all sides with 1-inch-wide strips cut on the cross grain.

4 Using cup hooks, hang one narrow metal curtain rod where ceiling and wall meet. Hang another rod parallel to and 30 inches from first rod. Make sure the rods fit securely into the hooks. Drape canopy along wall and over both rods. Adjust canopy to swag as shown. Tack stuffed animals to the points.

COUNTRY COZY

Full of whimsy and old-fashioned warmth, country style brings heart and soul to any room, including the nursery. Although the style can feature pricey antiques and folk art, this nursery is proof that it's also achievable on a shoestring. Friendly patterns and cozy colors are the key.

CREATING A BUDGET STRETCHER

• **Wrap a room in scenic charm** without busting the budget by limiting pictorial wallpaper to a border. This bunny-themed paper circles the room about two-thirds of the way up the wall, entertaining the baby with an eyeful of picnicking bunnies. Bisecting the wall with a border also allows for the lower half to be decoratively painted with big cabana stripes—a wainscoting effect at much less the cost.

• **Create a custom look** by selecting a design from a children's collection that offers matching or coordinated crib linens, fabrics, wall coverings, curtains, and accessories. The bunny theme used here creates continuity. Classic themes last longer than fads. Here the color inspiration began with the wall-mounted quilt that serves as a focal point.

• **Be a good scout** to save money. A second-hand futon sofa, integrated into the room with new fabrics, makes a comfy time-out spot for parents. Search clearance sales for finds such as this nursery's new white changing table. Also inquire about purchasing floor models. For example, this new crib was sold at a special price as a floor model.

PAINT YOUR OWN STRIPES

There's more than one way to stripe a wall. Instead of applying a striped paper, which can add up in dollars and labor (especially when you tire of the paper and it's time for it to come down), learn the artful approach of paint. You'll need: painter's masking tape made for decorative painting, carpenter's level, measuring tape, latex wall paint, pencil, and paintbrushes (see pages 98–107 for painting tips).

ABOVE: *Charming looks begin with wallpaper borders, easy to apply and easy on the budget. Coordinate with matching linens and fabrics.* **PAGE 32:** *Create a cozy nursery with flea market finds or family hand-me-downs. Base colors on a quilt or favorite fabrics. A futon adds a spot for parent naps.*

• Decide how wide you want your stripes (probably from 2 to 4 inches for most rooms).

• Prime walls with a premium-bond primer. After they dry, paint on a white latex base coat. Allow it to dry to avoid smudging.

• Measure and mark stripes on the wall with a pencil, using the level to ensure straight lines. Don't erase or you'll smudge the wall.

• Mask off every other stripe with tape, as follows: Carefully mask the outer edge of each pencil mark with quality painter's masking tape. Tightly seal down the edge next to the pencil lines with your fingers to prevent the paint from bleeding through. Test a small area first to be safe.

• Paint the stripes of bare wall exposed in between the masked-off stripes. Use smooth, even strokes.

• After the color is applied, gently remove the tape (don't yank it) before the paint dries, being careful not to smear.

UP, UP, &AWAY

Not all nursery themes weather well. Those that don't soon end up too babyish for the room's maturing young occupant. But there is good news for parents who want a stimulating environment with staying power beyond infancy. Find a fantasy theme with ageless appeal.

PICK A TIMELESS THEME

This nursery's trompe l'oeil—French for "fool the eye" with decorative painting—walls of hot-air balloons soar through a sky filled with fluffy white clouds. The balloon and cloud theme offers more longevity than more common nursery motifs, such as teddy bears, clowns, or trains. The pale cloud-infused walls don't become tiresome as they are subtle in pattern and palette. Almost like a neutral background, the walls offer wide-open options for introducing other colors and patterns in fabrics, which means you can change things as the child grows up. (See pages 22 and 75 for instructions on painting clouds.)

FURNISHINGS TO GROW

Only one furniture piece—the crib—needs replacing to transform the nursery into a youth room. The other furnishings work equally well for an infant or even a teen. The chest of drawers isn't age-restricted; painted white, it offers the softness desired for a nursery. The dresser snuggles up to the twin bed as a side table, displaying photos and personal accessories. (During the toddler stage remember to keep breakables out of reach.)

SOFTNESS UNDERFOOT

Other features such as the creamy wall-to-wall carpet are appropriate throughout the

ABOVE: *Young but not babyish, the nursery features the easy-to-live-with ballooning theme. Classic draperies allow a nursery to convert to a guest room or study.*
RIGHT: *French phrases on this pillow prove that grown-up fabrics translate for babies.*

child's development. The soft carpet is an ideal surface for the baby just learning to crawl and walk. Its demure good looks also offer a grown-up flavor older children can appreciate. There's only one drawback: Inevitable spills and stains from an active child mean high maintenance on a light, single-color carpet. For most wear for your dollar, make sure any carpet you buy has been treated to be stain-resistant. Though looped carpet isn't as soft and lush as cut pile, it wears longer. Extra padding also makes carpet feel softer underfoot or under the knees of a crawling baby.

ABOVE: *Clouds and balloons—themes that last well into childhood—soothe the senses in this serene nursery. Recessed lighting on dimmers and a lamp give balanced illumination. A comfortable rocker with cushions is a necessity.*

NECESSITIES

THE ESSENTIALS. Tons of furnishings aren't necessary for a well-stocked nursery. In fact, the fewer the better. Efficient essentials free up floor space for walking to soothe your infant to sleep and for play areas later. Our recommendations include:

• **Crib and mattress (see safety guidelines on page 27). You may be tempted to bring your newborn into bed with you, but a crib is safer. You'll also be grateful later on that you started the routine of your baby sleeping alone early; you'll both be better rested.**

• **Crib bumper pad. This provides a soft buffer between your baby and the hard crib rails once he or she starts rolling or scooting over. Be careful once your baby is pulling up; a climber might use the bumper pad like a ladder to get out of the crib.**

• **3 or 4 fitted crib sheets, 2 mattress pads, 1 crib quilt, 3 receiving blankets (no pillow during the baby's first year).**

• **Chest of drawers or built-in drawers beneath crib.**

• **Storage for diapers and wipes, changing pads, baby towels and wash cloths, and other bath/ grooming products. A changing table is ideal, but a closet shelf also works.**

• **Locating the rocker in the nursery reduces the distance you have to carry your sleeping infant to put him or her down to sleep.**

• **Extra: A twin bed or daybed adds a resting spot for a parent caring for a child and can double as a bed for visitors if space is tight. See pages 14–17 for examples of double-duty nurseries.**

CIRCUS
CIRCUS

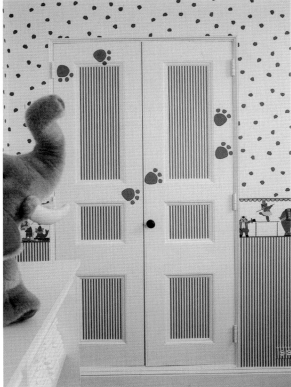

With runaway monkey footprints dotting its walls, a circus-themed nursery inspires high spirits and a sense of fun from infancy on. Vital ingredients include a wall treatment of hand-painted monkey feet plus three different wallpaper patterns: candy stripes for the lower wall, abstract dots at the top, and a circus border that runs just above the crib for baby's easy viewing pleasure. As the child matures, replace the juvenile border with one for an older child, paint over the footprints, and keep the stripes and dots. Repeating the red-and-white striped paper on the closet-door panels customizes the look. All that remains for big-top entertainment are a trapeze artist monkey—a clever alternative to the more expected above-crib mobile—and a carousel-style rocking horse.

PAGE 36: This valance pulls together the nursery's palette and motifs in one abbreviated treatment. It repeats the stripes of the wallpaper but in black instead of red, and its trim reinforces the room's reds and dots. The valance deliberately mimics a balloon shade, but is an easy-to-make fake. To achieve the full puffy look, simply mount the valance on two tension rods in two rod pockets and stuff with inexpensive bridal netting from a fabric store. For privacy, back the valance with shades or blinds that go into hiding when not in use.

PEACEABLE KINGDOM

A hideaway in the trees tops every child's fantasy list, so why not start the dreaming early with a treehouse-themed nursery? An absence of architecture is no drawback—in fact, it's a plus. Start with a plain white room, then build your own architecture with real wood boards for dimension. Add fancifully painted walls sprouting tree branches and chattering squirrels for sheer fun. (For more information on painting techniques, see pages 98–107; for help in finding an artist, see page 90.)

A combination of boards and hand painting gives this nursery its treehouse charm. As an alternative, substitute wallpaper borders and murals. Paint window frames forest green or bark brown for the woodsy theme.

A treehouse nursery doesn't even require a second-story location. But a window with a view is a plus as a starting point for the nature theme that thrives inside. Even when the red maple outside this nursery window drops its leaves, the indoor branches hold their color all year long.

QUICK-CHANGE TABLE

If a bland box bedroom can become a treehouse treasure, it's an easy order to transform an existing dresser, chest, drop-leaf desk, or even a countertop into a changing table for your baby. All that's needed is a furnishing wide enough for a baby that's waist-high or taller (to save your back) that can be cleared of clutter. Top it with a standard rubber pad and fitted cloth cover to soften the surface. (Special guardrails and restraining straps increase safety, but never leave your baby unattended on the table.)

THROWING A CURVE ON STORAGE

• **Curve the edges** when building storage shelves with exposed ends. Or, let your storage shelves span the entire wall, fitting both ends into the two facing walls. (Shelf spans should be no more than 30 to 36 inches, depending on weight, between supports; for more shelving how-tos, see page 11.)

• **Keep lower storage open,** especially when your baby is small. Cabinet doors are invitations for smashed fingers.

• **Store heavy or breakable items** above a baby's reach. Anything stored on lower shelves should be safe for your baby to grab.

GOING INTO NEUTRAL

When your aim is a nursery that soothes like a lullaby, consider a neutral color scheme—especially one on the pale side of the palette. Soft on the eye, creamy ivories and taupes create the perfect kind of stress-free serenity you want for you and your baby. Because such hues aren't sticky-sweet or predictable color choices, they age well without becoming dated as your baby grows up. The darker neutrals—blacks, browns, and grays—also are cocooning colors, but their depth carries an edge inappro-

priate for an infant. Use them only as accents on a few natural-finish wood furnishings, but not on the ceiling, walls, and windows. Reserve those larger surfaces for the pale neutrals, subtle enough to take patterns without looking busy, as these harlequin-patterned, faux-painted walls prove. Also consider the "new" neutrals for other pacifying palettes. Sage green and pale peach or muted rose, lightened with white, work as neutrals. Use fabrics and such touches as the bright balloon for stimulating contrast.

PAINTERLY

HARLEQUIN PAINT

Pattern. Inside the painted-on harlequin pattern, left and bottom left, walls wear decorative sponge painting. This results in an overall look of free-form spontaneity, even within the diamond shapes. Supply list:

   1 gallon flat latex beige paint

   1 quart or gallon (depending on room size) semigloss taupe

   Pints of semigloss paints in contrasting colors for tiny dots

   Natural sea sponges

   Erasable pencil

   Straightedge

   Stiff artist's brush

1 First paint the entire wall area with a flat latex beige. Then apply a taupe wash (3 parts taupe paint diluted with 1 part water) over it with a natural sea sponge. Avoid circle shapes for a greater sense of random movement.

2 Measure off guide points for the harlequin patterns with an erasable pencil. Connect the guide dots with a straightedge and pencil lines to make the harlequin outline.

3 Using a stiff artist's brush, outline every other diamond with a darker shade of taupe paint, this time in a semigloss finish. Then paint inside the diamonds with an artist's brush.

4 For detailing, use contrasting colors for tiny dots at the tangents. (For more on specialty paint finishes and techniques, see pages 104–107.) Don't worry about your painting being precise and entirely inside the lines; the charm is in the look of hand painting.

PAGE 40: *A wicker daybed, versatile in a small space, won't ever be outgrown. Neither will the display shelves and plates.*

ABOVE: *Built-ins flanking the window maximize storage, especially in rooms where space is tight.*

RIGHT: *Paint in a neutral palette, without an obvious theme, and your nursery will not only work through childhood, but it also will easily convert into a guest room or office. Use fabrics and accents to adapt the low-key look to changing styles and needs.*

BOLD & BRIGHT

Your own color preferences are bound to turn up in your baby's nursery. Think of the hours that you'll spend in the room, and you'll see why you should choose colors that suit your eye and psyche. Some might find the neutral palette on page 41 serene, but parents who prefer more contrast—or a sunny visual treat after the occasional short night—might prefer something more stimulating. If that nursery's mission was to rock-a-bye baby, this one rocks around the clock as a wake-up call.

Two factors influence this scheme: the mom's favorite color (purple) and overall fondness for vivid hues and the fact that babies are stimulated by high-contrast palettes. Newborns respond best to black and white and older babies to brighter, contrasting hues. The free-hand stripes that climb these walls offer something for everyone: the clear-cut contrast needed for the newborn, a dose of lemony yellow for the tot, and purple for the mom. A red ceiling border outlined in teal blue frames freehand orbiting stars and suns. Furniture gets custom coats of decorative paint, repeating the wall's motifs and hues, and adding a few extras just for the fun of it.

ABOVE: *Hand painting, not perfect lines, gives charm to this decorated chest, a flea market find. Polyurethane protects the piece from the rigors of everyday use.*
PAGE 42: *Forget any "rules" about nursery colors. If you like bright, bold colors, such as this purple and citrus yellow, enjoy them. Balance with white and naturals to keep from overpowering your nursery and baby.*

CELESTIAL
STARS AND STRIPES.
   1 gallon white flat latex paint
   Erasable pencil
   Yardstick; carpenter's measuring tape
   Pints of bright colors (semigloss) for stripes and details
   Water-based polyurethane
• **Before beginning the decorative painting, paint the walls and ceiling with a white flat latex.**
• **Start the freehand stripes by measuring off guidelines with a pencil. It helps if you use a yardstick and carpenter's measuring tape to designate the stripes, which you mark with pencil. Paint freehand over the pencil lines.**
• **Practice freehand stars on scrap particleboard or plywood first, to perfect the look you like. If you can't master the stars, make a star stencil pattern, then place the stencil on the wall and trace around it with pencil. Finally, paint between the lines.**
TREASURE CHEST. Paint a junk piece of furniture or a flea market find with the room's same bold scheme: Here's how:
• **Paint the chest with a base coat of white flat latex.**
• **Paint on details with small, stiff artist's brushes.**
• **After the chest dries, seal it with a water-based polyurethane top coat. TIP■ To get just the right custom colors, take a sample of your favorite color into your paint store. With their new computerized mixing abilities, the store will be able to replicate the exact color you want.**

ROOMS WITH STYLE

BETWEEN TOT AND TEEN, children's interests and needs change as fast as their shoe sizes. But the rooms in this chapter keep pace with ideas designed for fun and learning. One bright example is our undersea adventure—a joy for any child who loves the ocean and beach. Turn the page for how-to tips.

JOY IN THE
DEEP BLUE SEA

If painting is your thing or you want to give it a whirl, this watery adventure is the place to begin. Or, if you like the look but don't have time, an art student or art teacher can tackle the job. (For how to find an affordable artist/decorative painter, see page 90.)

If you're ready for this adventure, here's how:

• *When a motif is as elaborate as the one shown here, it pays to plan.* To make sure furniture or planned built-ins don't obscure whimsical art, measure and arrange what will go in the room.

• *Begin by looking through magazines,* coloring books, and books about the sea for pictures of a variety of ocean creatures. Practice drawing fish and sea creatures to simplify motifs and shapes.

• *Gather your supplies.* For this wall treatment, you'll need latex paints, a paint roller, artist's acrylics in a selection of bright colors, artist's paintbrushes, and painter's tape.

• *Forget the boundaries of wall and ceiling.* Brush the wall junction, the imaginary water line between a sky blue ceiling and deep ocean blue walls, in latex paints. Paint the sky first with light blue latex paint, then mask off the perimeter with painter's tape and roll on dark blue paint.

• *Outline* stylized fish with white chalk on the dark blue background, fill in with paint, and outline again with black permanent markers. Vary the sizes, shapes, and colors of the fish for interest.

• *Use natural sponges* and white and green latex paint to create the underwater bubbles and foam. Sponge-paint the ceiling clouds in gray, white, and blue tones. (For more on clouds and sponge techniques, see pages 22, 75, and 103.) Paint and sponge coral and seaweeds if you want more detail. Seal walls with flat polyurethane.

• *Hang netting* anchored with toy lobsters and crabs for a lighthearted window treatment. Miniblinds control light.

• *For extra fun,* paint the sun motif and illuminate it with a boxed fluorescent strip or incandescent strip from a home center.

ABOVE: *With such an elaborate theme, keep furniture and upholstery as simple as possible and in the same color family. Blue is the obvious choice for this watery retreat. Shop military surplus stores for finds such as this real diver's helmet.*

PAGE 46: *Finish the seagoing adventure in style. An old trunk makes the perfect treasure chest when your child is old enough to open and close it safely.*

LEAVING THE NURSERY BEHIND

Looking for design direction, this little cowpoke's bedroom headed West—in spirit, that is. It corrals a herd of fun fabrics, from cowboy denim to bucking bronco and cow prints, that inspire every element in this back-at-the-ranch scheme. Here's how to create a ranch retreat:

• **Select a coverlet fabric with a rich red background.** Have wall paint custom-mixed to match. Wallpaper the ceiling with a starry night motif (see pages 108–109 for how-to tips). Add a comfortable braided cotton rug for playing on the floor.

• **Hire a professional sign painter to set the walls to music.** Or, try your hand at lettering (see stenciling tips on pages 106–107). Lyrics from a favorite cowboy tune sashay around the room.

• **Upholster an adult-size easy chair** in the cow-print cotton. It's perfect for curling up with Mom or Dad for a bedtime story. Repeat the fabric on a sham for an oversize bed pillow.

FROM CRIB TO BED

When it's time for the first big bed, 2-year-olds may deliver the wake-up call by crawling out of the crib and heading for Mom and Dad's room to say, "Good morning." Or you might awake one day to find your little early bird playing in the living room. These nonverbal cues signal blossoming independence.

Although 2 to 2½ years is a common age for the transition, it could happen at 3 years. You don't need to rush it. When you make the switch is

Crisp white crown molding and shutters set off a happy trails bedroom that satisfies the youngster's love of bright colors. Add real cacti in terra-cotta pots and a cowboy lamp for authentic accents.

up to you and your child. Observe your child's physical development; stronger toddlers may escape the crib at 18 months. The Sleep Products Safety Council advises that toddlers 35 inches tall are ready for that first bed. Children with older siblings may show more—and earlier—interest in moving to a grown-up bed.

SHOPPING SENSE

THE FIRST BIG BED. Give your child's first real bed special thought because it's a major investment. The right choice can last through the teen years. Shop with your child. Check the products' warranties, construction, materials, and safety labels. You'll both want to bounce on the mattress to test for comfort. Before you buy, consider these tips:

• Twin beds with headboards measure 75×44 inches; mattresses are 75×39. Double beds with headboards are 75×59 inches; mattresses are 75×54. Twin-size sleep sets are the most popular choice. However, bedding industry statistics show more parents are choosing full-size beds for children because they allow room for growth and are roomier for parent and child during talks and stories.

• For safety, the frame should have rounded edges. If it has spindles or slats in the headboard, make sure spaces are too narrow for a child's head to get caught.

• Whether you choose an inner-spring, foam, flotation, or futon mattress, it also should fit snugly into the bed frame with no space between to catch little hands and feet. Twin inner-spring mattresses should have more than 200 coils; full-size mattresses more than 300.

• Detachable side rails discourage climbing and may help your child feel more secure.

• Space-saving extras, such as a trundle bed for sleep-overs or headboard storage, may be important to you.

• Think carefully about an antique bed. Some are short and narrow and won't last long for a tall child. Be sure the frame is sturdy and smooth; reglue, if necessary.

To gauge your child's interest in making the change, talk it over. Together, look at children's rooms in magazines and take your child along to shop for a bed. Let your child choose sheets and pillowcases; you pick outer bedding in timeless colors and patterns. After you make the bed, add some "old friends" from the crib.

"If joy you win, you must share it. For happiness was b

twin.'
Lord Byr

TWICE THE FUN

As fresh as a day in the country, this softly feminine room shared by twins wraps airy furnishings in happy colors. Not everything is spanking new here—a clever paintbrush just makes it look that way.

• *Before repainting,* the old wood pencil-post beds looked more colonial than cottage in style. White paint fixed that. The flowerpot comforters provided color cues for the beds, which were perked up with stripes painted on the posts and big fat polka dots on the headboards and footboards. (For furniture-painting tips, see page 43.)

• *The palette-setting comforter fabric* works perfectly for grade-schoolers, echoing children's drawings of bright-hued pots and blooms.

• *Old-fashioned gingham* in a peppermint red backs the reversible comforters. The gingham encores in chair cushions, shams, and in bed skirts trimmed in sweet eyelet.

Displayed in acrylic shadow boxes, each little girl's mementos— christening dress, birth announcement, bib, and booties—personalize the wall above the beds. Miniprint fabric, pinned on so it can be changed later, covers box backgrounds. Frame shops can make boxes to specifications.

• *Porch-style pieces of white wicker* enhance the classic cottage feel. For an easy-to-clean surface, a glass top protects the low chest between the beds. Smoothed, rounded edges ensure safety.

• *Painted in a bows-and-blooms motif,* a child's table and mix-and-match chairs stand ready for teatime. The cotton rag rug adds a soft touch.

• *In keeping with the crisp cottage theme,* blue painted walls balance the wallpapered ceiling. (For tips on papering a ceiling, see pages 110–111.)

• *Making the scheme multicolored* translates into versatility. Any new toy or treasure—no matter what the hue—blends right in, and that's important when two collectors share a room.

PICK A NOVELTY PRINT

An allover print fabric featuring rainbow-colored pots and flowers puts the twins' bedroom in a garden mood. Avoid too-juvenile patterns your child will quickly outgrow. A novelty-print fabric easily sets a decorating palette or a room theme. Use only one so your motif doesn't have competition. For variety, mix in stripes or checks that repeat a color of the print.

Gear your fabric choice to your child's interests and pick one together. Popular cotton or cotton-blend fabrics with teapots, teacups, and English pottery, or even grown-up toile make delightful accents. So do fabrics with ships, animals, stars, moons, and clouds. As an alternative, use a print for a skirted table and pillows.

A PLACE TO PLAY

Get ready to learn and create. This playroom takes advantage of often-overlooked space: a large landing at the top of the stairs.

• *Patchwork walls tie together* the playroom's varied colors and the primary palettes of the three adjacent children's rooms. These crayon-bright blocks in red, green, yellow, blue, and black are solid-hued wallpapers. The big squares are 22×22 inches, and the black squares at the corners are 4×4 inches. Apply squares one at a time to get the color mix right. (For more on wallpaper, see pages 108–111.)

• *Upholstered in striped canvas,* the adult-size seating treats the playroom to family room comfort. It's the get-together spot where parents join children for bedtime stories and television viewing. The little painted table doubles as a coffee table and a surface for drawing.

• *Although it's custom-designed* as a handsome piece of freestanding furniture, the heavy-duty wall unit is built in so there's no danger of it tipping over. Open and closed storage organizes toys and games, plus entertainment gear. There's a special drawer for checkers, cars, and hopscotch pieces needed for the games painted on the floor.

• *Wall sconces and recessed ceiling fixtures* brighten the scene. The combination is a safer choice than floor or table lamps, which rambunctious children may knock down, and eliminates cords they might trip over.

• *Tongue-in-groove wainscoting* with a washable painted finish protects lower walls from sticky fingers and out-wears gypsum board in an active space.

PAINT TRICK

• *Ceiling.* It's no wonder imaginations soar in this playroom. "You can fly!"—a snippet of the script from *Peter Pan*—floats the length of the ceiling, courtesy of a sign painter. Before the quote was brushed on, the ceiling got a blue sky paint job with airbrushed clouds. Embellish sky ceilings in children's bedrooms and playrooms with a painted sun, rainbow, and clouds or a nighttime moon and stars. Write the child's name to look as if it were done by a skywriter plane. Use stencils for stars, lettering, or

ABOVE: *The fun is coming up with your own idea. Outline it first, then paint it freehand with enamels. Sealed floors will have to be stripped before painting.*

PLANNING

PLAYROOM BASICS. Consider
these child-pleasing decorating ideas
that you will like, too:

• **Have fun with the backdrop.** Paint
walls a jazzy color or each wall a
different bold hue with scrubbable
latex paints. If you're not artistic,
roll on a fanciful mural of vinyl-
coated wall covering.

• **Get personal.** Enlarge your child's
favorite birthday or vacation photos
for poster-size wall art. Incorporate
the child's name in accents.

• **Choose hard-surface floors, such**
as vinyl composition tile or
polyurethane-protected wood, for
flooring; add a piece of bound
carpet for floor games.

• **Slipcover seating in durable,**
washable fabrics, such as cotton
chenille, canvas, and denim. Add
giant pillows with washable covers
for floor seating.

• **Install built-in storage wherever**
possible. Put bookcases under the
stairs, wrap cabinetry around walls,
tuck entertainment centers beneath
sloped attic ceilings, and hinge
window seats for toy storage.

• **Hang Homasote, a tackable board,**
as a surface for pinning up treasures
and artwork. It comes in 4×8 sheets
from building supply or home
centers and can be covered with
bright-colored fabric.

• **Create a play spot in the kitchen**
or den with toys and art supplies
on low shelves in a nearby cabinet.
Run storage areas and a countertop
with a kneehole for a desk across
one end of the family room for art
projects and homework.

• **Add a let's-pretend spot,** *page 52,*
by spiffing up an old trunk and filling
it with dress-up clothes from garage
sales or the attic. Add safety hinges
so the lid doesn't fall on fingers.

ABOVE: *As exuberant in its design as the children who love it, this top-of-the-stairs playroom makes a busy hub for the whole family. With no-fuss painted finishes and fabrics and lots of options for creative play, the house rule here is just have fun.*

other graphics. (For cloud painting techniques, see pages 22, 75, and 103; for more painting techniques, see pages 98–107.)

• *Floor.* No need to ask directions to the laundry. Just follow the socks, jeans, and T-shirts an artist painted on the floor of this playroom with an adjacent laundry. Now the floor can be a real mess and still look great. These siblings picked the clothing for the artist's masterpiece. There's more floor art in the playroom proper. The artist painted a hopscotch grid, a checkers board, and an around-the-room racetrack in oil-based enamels on the wood floor before it was sealed. Paint game boards on tabletops, too, for convenient play. (For tips on hiring a decorative painter, see page 90; for floor painting techniques, see page 100.) Caution: Consider painted floors permanent. Later, for a more adult look, the floors will have be repainted or stripped and refinished.

ULTIMATE FUN ZONE

Bright and open, this sunny playroom features activity centers, so what's on the agenda is every child's choice. It could be puzzles on the hardwood, Monopoly on the rug, or art at the easel. The stepped window seat, piled with pillows for story time, doubles as a toy box.

Planning such centers within a playroom nurtures creativity, but to make them work and play successfully, consider your child's age and interests.

• *Provide multiple surfaces for projects and play,* but keep overall furnishings to a minimum and floor space open. Built-in units for play surfaces and storage can help accomplish this. Or, have a table and chairs for play and a separate desk for study.

• *Remember, wet play areas* for painting and finger paints should have hard-surface floors and well-sealed wood or laminate tables or countertops.

• *Consider space and storage for electronic equipment.* Tuck gear behind closed—and locked—doors to protect it from misuse.

• *Create warm and fuzzy spots* with rugs on the floor and an adult-size overstuffed chair for snuggling.

• *Zone storage to specific activities.* For example, stow art supplies in the wet zone, books near the cozy area, and flash cards by the desk.

Combine play and study areas for a playroom your child won't soon outgrow. An easel gives a young artist display space.

SHARED SPACES

Sharing a room with a sibling can teach lessons that last a lifetime—compromise, cooperation, negotiation, and respect for others' possessions. "Their" room should be a fun place to play and relax, but just because they share a space doesn't mean their needs and tastes are the same. Here are some ways to foster sharing while nurturing their individuality:

• *Don't insist that everything be coordinated.* One family pleased two young room-sharers by making copies of the room's floor plan and asking each child to color it. One child preferred yellow and the other red, so those colors decorated their own spaces.

• *Sharing works best if children are the same sex and as close in age as possible.* Don't pair up a toddler with a 9-year-old whose Lego pieces and tiny toys could pose a choking hazard for the little one.

• *Carve out personal space for each child.* Give the budding artist a tackable surface for hanging artwork and the little collector a shelf for display.

• *To boost self-esteem, let each child pick* colors, patterns, and bed linens to identify their spaces and possessions.

• *Minimize clutter with multipurpose furniture,* such as an armoire for a computer, rolling bins that fit under beds, and storage headboards. For harmony, color-code each child's bins.

• *If major storage must be shared,* give each child a private spot with a lock for stowing treasures. It could be a box, an old trunk, or a dresser drawer.

ABOVE: *With the addition of twin beds, a tentlike attic turned into a top-of-the-house tepee. To provide more play space center stage for a game table and chairs, the crisp white metal sleepers hug the walls beneath the angled ceiling. A wing chair and bookcase are set on the diagonal in the corners. Design elements—a quilt-motif carpet, rugged plaid bedspreads, and horsey accents—conjure up Wild West spirit.*

RIGHT: *These bright-blue metal bunks offer a versatile choice: Instead of the conventional stacked configuration, each bed has a different view. The ladder at a comfortable climbing angle and sturdy upper guardrails prevent falls.*

ABOVE: *In this all-boy retreat, the natural-finish wood bunk beds blend with the room's rustic furnishings, cowboy-print linens, and Western accents. To camouflage the room's badly cracked plaster, walls are covered in low-cost composite paneling and painted to look like weathered barn boards. To achieve this finish, lightly brush red paint over gray paneling, allow to dry, then brush on white paint. Practice your technique on scrap wood. For more on painting, see pages 98–107.*

ACCOMMODATIONS

BUNK BED SAFETY. Check product warranties and labels outlining proper use. Look for a manufacturer who stands behind the bunk bed for its lifetime. Ask whether the product meets the voluntary safety standards set by the American Society of Testing and Materials. Make sure top and bottom posts fasten together.

• Shop for beds made of strong, durable materials with smooth, rounded edges. Shake the unit to make sure it's stable.

• Determine that side rails are bolted on. Guardrails should be difficult to remove or require release of a fastening device; they should run the length of the upper bed on both sides.

• Make sure there's no more than 1 inch between mattress and bed frame and mattress-supporting slats are screwed into the sides of the beds. Mattress should be at least 5 inches below the top of the guardrails.

• Make sure the bottom bunk is roomy enough for sitting up.

• Look for a unit with a ladder that's securely attached at a comfortable angle for climbing. If it's removable, it should be easy to reattach. Steps should be 10 inches wide and have a 12-inch vertical space between each one.

• Check occasionally that screws and bolts are tightened.

• Keep all assembly material. Leave the safety information sticker on the unit.

• Never allow children younger than 6 to sleep on the top bunk. Allow only one person at a time on the top bunk and never allow horseplay up there.

ROOM ARRANGEMENTS THAT GROW

Keeping room-sharers happy depends on what furnishings you select for them and how you arrange the room. Younger children enjoy common play areas, but for peaceful coexistence, carve out separate but equal areas for sleep and solitary pursuits, such as reading.

PLAN A: CHILDHOOD YEARS

This room arrangement, *near right*, is adapted for 6- to 11-year-olds and makes privacy and storage priorities in the shared space.

• *For more privacy,* the beds are moved to opposite sides of the room and are on different levels. One's a loft-style bed.

• *A dresser fits* under the loft for additional storage. The small storage units double as bedside tables.

• *For hobbies and projects,* done together or individually, a colorful table and chairs in one corner offer plenty of space.

• *Storage by the table* holds art supplies, books, and other materials for this activity and homework area.

• *Removing closet doors* and substituting colorful shower curtains frees up more space.

PLAN B: THE TEEN YEARS

As the sibling roommates edge into their teens, their room needs to work even harder when it comes to privacy and expanded study space for homework.

Just by rearranging some of the same furniture, the room they've shared since childhood is transformed to handle more grown-up pursuits.

• *To create separate study areas and minimize distractions,* the beds are moved so there's private space at opposite ends of the room.

• *The desk at the end of the loft bed* has storage

beneath the bed and a corner bulletin board. The other desk has expanded vertical shelving around it for shared library space.

• *The table and chairs are eliminated* to accommodate the new bed arrangement.

• *Because lively colors* in the furnishings, floor covering, and bed linens are as pleasing to teens as they are to younger children, the palette stays the same.

• *For added privacy,* closet doors are returned.

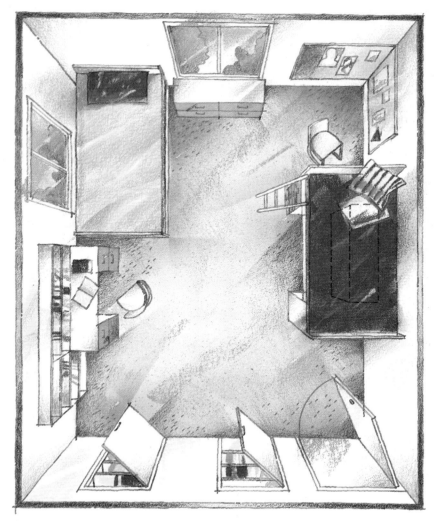

◀ PLAN A ▲ PLAN B

PEACEFUL DIVISION. Dividing one space into two cozy domains doesn't require costly remodeling, but it does take creativity. As you plan room arrangements, brainstorm with your children and incorporate their ideas and needs. Whatever dividers you choose, they should be as flexible as possible so each child's space opens for sharing or closes for privacy. Also make sure that dividers allow heat, air, and light to filter adequately into both sides of the room. These items help divide a space:

• Modular, stackable bookcases.
• A large chalkboard on casters.
• A row of low storage units, such as plastic bins or cubes, lined up across the floor.
• A shelving unit, with shelves on both sides, that stretches from the floor to the ceiling.
• A two-sided storage unit with closed and see-through shelving.
• A whole or half wall made from wallboard.
• Well-attached, ceiling-mounted blinds or curtain panels for safe privacy (unlike floor screens, which can topple over).

CRATE IDEAS! Colorful plastic crates make high-function building blocks when you need to define boundaries in shared space. Use crates to create a room divider-bookcase with access from both sides. Or, stack two pairs and add a plywood top for an instant desk with storage, *left*. Lash crates together with plastic garbage bag ties or ties provided with the crates. Fill with books and toys, placing heavier objects at the bottom.

ABOVE: A young resident can enjoy this retreat with a garden view, thanks to the hand-painted mural that picks up the picket theme from her charming bed. If she outgrows her interest in gardening, it will be easy to brush on a change of scene.

RIGHT: A room-for-two gathers rosy pink-print fabrics and garden-theme furnishings. As an alternative to these custom-made beds, paint or stencil bunnies or garden motifs on headboards.

HER OWN SECRET GARDEN

An artist's mural and a bouquet of floral fabrics transform an ugly duckling bedroom into a beauty that's sure to live happily ever after.

• *Start with a whimsical vegetable patch theme,* anchored by a custom-made picket-fence bed. But there are no pointy pickets on the bed to cause bumps and bruises; headboards and footboards are gently curved and fence post ends have rounded finials. Check with a local furnituremaker if you'd like to commission a similar rounded design.

BUDGET STRETCHER: Here's how to make a straight picket-fence headboard. Measure the width of a standard bed frame in inches and divide by 3; this determines the number of precut 1×3-inch wood pickets needed. Cut the pickets 48 inches long; for supports, cut two pickets the same width as the bed frame. Lay supports 12 inches apart on a flat surface. Position pickets on top of supports and nail in place. If desired, whitewash the headboard with equal parts white paint and water for an aged effect. (Some larger home centers sell pickets with tops already cut for details.)

• *Paint the walls soft yellow* and add a gardener's fantasy mural of a vine-covered picket fence alongside a working plot. (For more on mural painting techniques, see pages 102–103. For ideas on hiring an art student to paint your motif, see pages 90–91.)

• *What would any garden be without flowers?* Dress the bed in a mix of country fresh prints in purple, blue, yellow, and green—a palette that links the room's accessories.

THE PINK BEDROOM

Vegetable garden motifs, abloom with rosy hues and dainty prints, abound in this garden spot.

• *Instead of more costly wallpaper,* a trellis-motif border accents the crown molding and painted walls.

• *Flowing curtains,* tied back with plaid bows, match the comforter fabric. It's a designer look doable with coordinated collections of sheets and bedding. Adding ribbons or fabric bows quickly dresses ready-made treatments and introduces girlish touches.

• *A diminutive bistro table and chairs,* dressed up with painted-on flowers, give the young owners a spot for tea with their dolls and for drawing projects.

THE SPORTING LIFE

Catch some team spirit. Do The Wave. Create a room for your young sports fan that's a crowd-pleaser with a future. There's no space to spare in this little stadium, but locker-gray laminate built-ins maximize every inch.

• **Go with a bed that adds storage** and sleep-over potential. There's a trundle bed underneath it, and the ledges that wrap around the bed have sections that open up for blanket storage and stationary surfaces for display.

• **Angle the desk** across a corner to free up floor space; design a desk top deep enough so it can become a computer workstation later on. (For more on computer and study areas, see pages 72–73.)

• **Add special perks for your jocks.** Next to the locker-room closet, there's a players' bench and, above it, a skybox in the stepped-up built-ins; bench sections have hidden drawers for storage. The top-level skybox has enough room for red-clad futon seating, more storage in plastic bins, and a small television. After all, who wants to miss The Big Game?

• **Paint walls pale gray** so your fan can personalize the room with pennants and posters of favorite teams and stars. For easy and inexpensive art, attach multiple sports trading cards on mat board with double-stick tape. Then frame the collage and hang it on the wall. Framed photos of sports heroes make easy-to-do accents.

• **Choose gray-and-white striped,** low-loop carpeting for its mini-gridiron look.

• **Draft sports-themed accessories** to heighten the fun. Big, squishy baseball and basketball pillows are great loungers on the bed. Team logo tins add color and storage. In the room shown, a real football helmet, sports action figures, and a bat-and-ball lamp add to the fun.

UPPER RIGHT: *Built-ins score big points in this young fan's room. The bed includes a pull-out trundle bed for a teammate to sleep over; the desk angles into a corner to save space; open walls and shelves display trophies.*

RIGHT: *Instead of painting doors to look like lockers, dry-mount a poster on foam core and hang for instant art.*

THE LOCKER ROOM

Give wood bifold closet doors the championship treatment with paint and real padlock handles. These were painted the green accent color that repeats around the trundle bed ledge and on the built-in storage. Use semigloss scrubbable latex paints for a long-wearing finish. If you've got an artistic streak, paint at least one of the lockers to look as though it's open, revealing sports gear. This whimsical painting features a variety of sports paraphernalia, even shoes and socks and it includes the fan's favorite sports drink and a basketball jersey with initials. Alternative: Stencil solid-color lockers with the names and numbers of sports heroes. (For stenciling tips, see pages 106–107.) The real padlock handles are hung on metal plates installed from the back of each door

GEAR UP

MAJOR LEAGUE BOOKENDS.
The sports gear on the shelves at *left* is permanently attached as bookends. It's important to use an all-purpose, heavy-duty glue suitable for the varied materials, such as leather on the balls and plastic on the football kicking tees. For the footballs, the tees are glued onto the shelf, then the footballs are glued onto the tees. To make a baseball glove stand up, make a wood base that can be screwed or glued to the shelf, then slip the glove over it.

HOME RUN HARDWARE.
Every detail in this bedroom has a sports connection. On the drawers, pulls are made from real baseballs, and handles are miniature bats. Include souvenir balls or bats or use those with favorite team logos.

To make the baseball pulls, drill a hole in the back of each ball. Cut a wood block to fit the hole and wood-glue the block into the ball. Hold the block over the drawer hole, and drill through the hole into the block. Run the screw through the drawer front into the ball. The screw length must be long enough to go through the drawer front and the wood block.

To make bat handles, buy wood dowel-like spacers, about 1½ inches long, that have threaded metal sleeves running through the center. Use two spacers per bat. Rout out two holes in each bat to fit one end of the spacers; the other end fits against the drawer. Choose screws long enough to go through the drawer fronts and the spacers into the bat.

ABOVE: *Not an inch of space goes to waste with clothing drawers built into the bed base and shelves for books and toys tucked beneath the steps. Dimmer controls are outside the beds so parents can supervise lights out.*

PAGE 65: *Compact and cozy, this laminate-clad bunk corrals sleepers and storage into a corner of the small room. Against the neutral gray and pale yellow backdrop, bright chintz coverlets and other accents splash on bold primary colors.*

SPACESHIP STYLE

Young imaginations take flight in this well-planned room that didn't let boxy dimensions and a lack of square footage spoil the fun. Raising the rafters to create a high-flying ceiling rescaled the space, a big new window brightens the area, and child-size furnishings leave plenty of floor space for play.

• *All systems are "Go"* in the command module-style bunk beds made of sleek laminates and designed with kid-friendly curves, playful cutout openings, and all the amenities any little space traveler could want. Instead of the usual bunk ladder, this unit has sturdy steps up to a big porthole entry so explorers can crawl into the upper level.

• *Each bed features* a rounded headboard shelf and recessed lights above the pillow for bedtime stories. Although the unit's sleepers are 6 feet long, they're customized for mattresses that are slightly narrower than single beds but just as comfy.

• *Interested in creating* a similar room? Working with curves, laminates, and custom furniture isn't do-it-yourself. For help, contact a designer or architect who specializes in residential work or call an experienced contractor.

ABOVE AND RIGHT: *For the most style with function, built-ins wrap around double-hung windows and the baseboard radiator. A frame of pine 2×4s, running the width of the room, boxes the radiator and creates a base for the plywood window seat and bookcases. The 12¼-inch-deep shelves are adjustable— as collections and books change through the years. To make the stars-and-moons grate along the bottom, cut shapes from 1×8 pine boards with a jigsaw; install boards 1 inch apart to allow heat circulation. To secure, attach the grate to the wall with wood glue. Countersink finishing nails with a nail set into wall studs and fill with wood putty.*

PAGE 67: *Pass up the typical youth bed with juvenile-theme sheets. Instead, dress an antique, ageless bed with lacy shams, a quilt, and mix-and-match grown-up linens.*

STAR BRIGHT

Dreaming of a fantasy room for your daughter? These tips will help you get started:

• **Base your color scheme** on a major feature of the room. Here it is based on the painted checkerboard trim woodwork in sunshine yellow, peach, green, blue, and pink. Repeat the colors in bed linens, a quilt, and balloon shade-style window valances.

• **Line the walls** with a Shaker peg railing mounted level with the tops of the doorways. To make and install the railing, cut a 1×3 pine board to length. Using wood glue, glue the board

to the wall. Cut two pieces of ½-inch-wide decorative molding the same length, then nail flush to the top and bottom of the railing with finishing nails. Drill holes for 3-inch-long Shaker pegs 5 inches apart; glue pegs into holes.

• **For the sky,** use your choice of dark blue and light blue latex paints. Roll or brush a base coat of dark blue on the ceiling and upper walls; let dry. Thin light blue paint with water. Wet a natural sea sponge, squeeze out water, and dip one side of the sponge into thinned paint. Blot excess paint on a newspaper, then dab paint randomly over the dark blue. Cut a smaller piece of sponge to blend thinned paint into corners and the ceiling line; let dry. (For another sky technique, see page 22.)

• **Hand-paint yellow stars** with white highlights over the sky. Or, cut a star stencil from acetate (available at crafts stores) and apply paints with a stencil brush. (For more detailed instructions on stenciling, see pages 106–107.)

• **For the checks** on a window seat, door, and window frames, use a stiff, flat brush in the width you want. Don't use a disposable foam brush. Apply a base coat of latex paint. Using a straightedge, lightly pencil in guidelines for the checked bands. Select paints in your favorite colors—five are used here—and dab them on. (For more on color combinations, see page 98.) Use as little paint as possible for each check; clean the brush in water between colors.

• **Stitch balloon-style valances.** For each valance, cut a piece of fabric twice the width and half the length of the window. Sew a casing along the top, hem the bottom, and add shirring tape down the center and sides. Mount the valance on a curtain rod, then pull and secure the shirring tape to the desired length. To finish, tack a decorative bow to the top center of the valance.

ROPING IT ALL TOGETHER

When the call of canyons and open ranges entices your cowboy or cowgirl, turn to these decorating ideas to create ranch house style. Though any room will do, the decoratively painted logs work well in the odd shapes of dormer rooms where young cowpokes often bunk. Here's how to put your own brand on a fun room:

• *Shop antiques and secondhand stores and auctions* for Western motif furniture. It's still possible to find pieces made in the 1940s and '50s. One or two pieces, such as an old rolltop desk, can set the mood.

• *Sew a duvet cover in cowboy print fabric* backed with denim. Or, purchase a comforter or duvet with a duvet cover in denim, corduroy, or plaid flannel. To quickly sew your own, measure and cut denim and decorative fabric the same size as your comforter, piecing if needed (second sheets from an outlet offer an economical option). With wrong side out, stitch front and back of the duvet together along three sides. Leave one short side open. For easy closing, hem raw edges, then stitch hook-and-loop fastening tape along top of the open side. Fold and insert the duvet or comforter. Press the tape closed.

• *Look for old pine chests for storage.* Or, age your own new unfinished pieces: Seal raw pine with a wood conditioner or shel-

lac; sand and stain with a honey shade. Allow the piece to dry and seal with furniture-quality paste wax.

• *Go over the top with finishing touches.* These exposed rafters, *below*, made from painted fence posts, display some of the cowboy collectibles that give the room its rootin'-tootin' character.

ABOVE: Use real rope to tie up denim window treatments hung on basic tension rods. PVC pipe in the bottom pockets keeps the denim taut.

LEFT: Carry over and expand your painting techniques when the bunkhouse includes a bath. Shop flea markets for old stirrups, Western art, and other just-for-fun accents.

PAGE 68: What would a roundup be without a fire? Or a bunkhouse without a fireplace? This one is entirely painted, down to the portable flame cutouts and the bricks.

THE WILD WEST

LOG IN. For the log cabin treatment, start with a white wall.
1 Measure wall height and divide by desired log height. Mark off the logs' horizontal borders in pencil, then brush borders with dark brown latex paint. To create the wood-grain effect between borders, use different shades of brown and beige latex paint.
2 Apply the browns and beiges with thin paintbrushes in varied widths from 1 to 4 inches. Use a dry-brush technique that entails dipping a dry paintbrush into a small amount of paint, then dragging it across the wall surface. Wipe the brush often with a cloth.
3 Use a brush to blend the varied shades into log borders. Add knots and striations to logs with dark brown paint. To make a knot, dip a brush into a small amount of paint and apply with a circular motion. Protect your masterpiece by rolling a coat of sun-blocking polyurethane over completely dry finished walls.
LEATHERY WALLS. The bath's walls begin with a base coat of rust brown flat latex paint applied with a roller and allowed to dry.
1 Thin white flat latex paint with water so it's translucent but not drippy. Use a sea sponge to lighten the rust brown base coat with variations of the thinned white mix; let dry.
2 Thin black flat latex paint with water and sponge it into crevices and corners to create shadows; let dry. Sketch cattle brands and flying rope details with white chalk; never use colored chalk because it bleeds.
3 Use brushes and acrylic paints to paint the beige rope and black brands. Seal with polyurethane.

ABOVE: *If the dance phase ends, don't despair. The wall works just as well as a teen's dressing mirror. Sponge-paint the rod to reflect the soft decor (for sponging tips, see page 104.)*

TOP RIGHT: *When space is limited, let a vanity double as a homework desk. Here gathered fabric tacked to the repainted desk hides drawer storage, but hook-and-loop tape strips would work as well.*

RIGHT: *Turn a twin bed sideways for a daybed look. For a no-sew bed hanging, suspend ready-made draperies from the ceiling molding.*

ROOM FOR DANCING

Mirror, mirror on the wall, how do you make a tiny bedroom the most fun of all? If your daughter dances, you have the answer—a mini dance studio. Fabric-covered walls glamorize the smallest space, and a ballet barre encourages practice.

• *For the look of upholstered walls* at a fraction of the time and cost, cut inexpensive dotted-Swiss fabric panels the same length as the wall plus 3 inches. For the width, measure the width of the wall, divide by fabric width, then multiply by 2. Using ½-inch seam allowances, stitch panels together along long sides. To finish, stitch 1-inch casings along top and bottom of fabric, then gather on narrow curtain rods mounted at the ceiling molding and baseboards.

• *Simulate an upholstered bed* with fabric: Cut decorative fabric (a small print works well) the same depth as the sides of the box springs, plus 1 inch, and four times the circumference. Cut a rectangle from sheeting the same size as top of box springs. Gather decorative fabric along long edges to fit around springs; secure gathers with running stitch. Stitch short edges of decorative fabric together, then stitch to all sides of sheeting, stitching contrasting cording in seams. Stitch cording around bottom of decorative fabric to finish. To cover each support, cut a 10-inch width of fabric the same length as the support, plus 5 inches. Stitch short sides together. Stitch ½-inch casing along both long edges. Thread cording through casings, place cover around support, then pull cording tight to fit around bottom of support. If desired, add stuffing to create a rounded effect.

• *Transform a white ceiling into a sunny sky.* Roll pale yellow latex paint over the white; press and remove plastic cellophane wrap over the wet paint to texture it. Sponge on white clouds. (For more on painting clouds, see pages 22, 75, and 103; for specialty painting techniques, see pages 98–107.)

• *Think through your dance studio.* If possible, the floor at the barre should be wood. Unless you are an experienced do-it-yourselfer, you'll want to have the mirrored wall and barre professionally installed. The barre here is a wood stairway handrail, similar to but heavier than a closet pole. Consult your child's dance teacher on the proper barre height, as it varies with the dancer's height. To make the barre adjustable, choose adjustable bracing hardware appropriate to the barre weight plus your daughter's weight. Anchor barre braces to wall studs on either side of the mirrored section so the barre can be raised.

HOME STUDY COURSE

This one

No "do your homework" reminders needed for the youngster who studies here. The math's still tricky, but a high-tech study wall makes working out the problems a pleasure.

• *This multipurpose bedroom* scores an A plus because it makes the most of a small space. The 14-foot-long window wall is obviously an asset, but wrapping sleek black built-ins around the view give it new function. With contemporary style and an easy-care black finish, this custom-designed wall unit appeals to grade-schoolers and teenagers alike.

• *The sprawling 6-foot-wide desk* provides lots of room for the all-important computer and printer and for spreading out papers and projects. File-and-supply drawers beneath are within easy reach.

• *Twin towers flank the desk* with open shelves for reference books and lower-level storage with doors. Lights at the top of each tower illuminate the shelves.

• *An adjustable desk chair* and computer keyboard shelf that stows beneath the desk top ensure the child won't soon outgrow this homework spot.

• *Lighting caters to the tasks at hand.* Recessed fixtures in the ceiling shine directly downward so they don't create glare on the computer screen. A small task lamp on the desk top balances light for reading.

PASTEL COLOR ROOM

Inspiring your student could be as easy as creating an inviting place for learning. Since your youngster knows his or her study needs best, design the homework spot together. First

determine what the priorities are: a computer, library shelves, space for sprawling art projects? Is your child left- or right-handed? That could determine the desk's layout. Let your child help pick the desk and color scheme.

• *Three scoops of sassy sherbet colors*—yellow, blue, and pink—make this window-nook study area on *page 73* stimulating and oh-so-personal because they're this student's favorites.

• *Instead of using a typical* window seat here, this room receives built-in function in the nook from a wide desk with

ABOVE: *Since picking the student's favorite color—bubble gum pink—for her desk, cracking the books became a lot more fun. The poufy window shades, "striped" in miniprint fabrics, pick up the pink and team it with two other pretty pastels.*

PAGE 72: *Black-and-white built-ins create a strong neutral background so the bedroom's lively accent colors of bold turquoise blue, pink, and yellow really pop. Zebra stripes painted on the closet door give this study spot a graphic and unexpected twist.*

drawer storage below on either side. The laminate desk teams bubble gum pink drawer fronts and sides with a lemony yellow top.

• *Swing-arm side lamps* mounted on the walls are a versatile lighting solution. They can be positioned where the student most needs the light and don't take up valuable desktop space. Located on both sides of the work surface, they don't create reflections on the computer screen that can cause eye strain. Avoid halogen desk lamps for younger children because they generate heat, which can be dangerous.

• *The handy computer keyboard shelf* resides out of the way under the desk top, then pulls up when it's needed.

ENLIGHTENED

STUDY SPOT BASICS. Measure available space before selecting furnishings for a homework area. If your student uses a computer, make sure there's adequate ventilation and light, enough grounded electrical outlets, a surge protector, and even a second phone line.

• Buy pieces that grow. Desk tops, chairs, and pull-out shelves for computer keyboards should adjust easily. Check construction and warranties before you buy and have your child test chairs for comfort. Standard desks are 30 inches high; computer stands are usually about 26 inches high.

• Consider modular furniture for a built-in look that's movable. Pair up storage pieces with a desk along a wall or even in a closet; slip a triangular desk top into a corner between bookshelves. Modulars don't have to be expensive, but they must be sturdy enough to support a computer.

• Paint unfinished furniture pieces, such as an armoire for a computer workstation with storage, in folk art colors to please grade-schoolers. Your teenager can repaint inexpensively for a new look. Use glossy or semigloss paints for an easy-clean finish; for durability, seal with polyurethane.

• Make a desk with brightly painted filing cabinets or stacked plastic crates as the end bases. Paint or stain a 4-foot-long, 1-inch-thick wood plank or a door that fits the depth of the cabinets or crates. Secure the crates together. Attach the plank to the tops of cabinets or crates with screws.

ABOVE AND PAGE 75: *Stuffed animals perch on the parapet of this bedroom castle that looks built-in but isn't. These modular units mix hardworking twin sleep spaces, storage, and multilevel play with the child's favorite storybook fantasy, Cinderella.*

Movable Castle

Thanks to cleverly designed modulars, the stroke of midnight finds this little Cinderella fan snoozing peacefully in her very own castle, perhaps dreaming of princes and pumpkins and sparkling glass slippers. Let a favorite once-upon-a-time tale inspire your child's room and imagination.

• *Everything had to squeeze* through the door in this 16×16-foot space, so the fantasy castle was built in pieces. The sections are constructed of medium-density fiberboard, then clad in sheets of gray speckled laminate that give the castle exterior a stonelike look. In design, it's like an indoor playground with crawl-spaces, cubbyholes, turret lookouts, and a walkway atop the castle wall reached via a sturdy stairway. There's lots of storage tucked in, too. ■TIP Working with detailed shapes and laminate isn't easy. A professional interior designer planned and supervised the work on this castle. Check with design students at a local college, junior college, or design school for cost-conscious help.

• *Two colors of carpet* create the moat of blue water at the castle base and the green land that stretches into the room.

• *The dreamy painted sky* comes

alive courtesy of sea sponges and paints. You'll need latex paint in white and sky blue and a white spray paint. Paint the ceiling blue, then spray on misty white clouds; don't let clouds get too filled in. Let dry. Sponge on layers of white clouds, dabbing the sponge on newspaper to remove excess paint before touching the ceiling. Let each layer dry before adding another. Painting a horizontal surface can be tricky, so practice your sponging technique on a drywall scrap first. (For more on painting clouds, see pages 22 and 103.)

• *Bedding and accent fabrics add* lively primary colors. The elegant chandelier plays to the storybook fantasy, yet provides bright general light. Look for small, affordable chandeliers on sale at home centers, lighting stores, or secondhand shops.

BATH BASICS

By carefully selecting durable surfaces and classic fixtures, you can design a bath that suits the little-red-schoolhouse crowd today and the bold-is-better teenagers tomorrow. Then splash on just-for-fun style with wall coverings, rugs, towels, and other accessories, all easy to change with your child's tastes. Here's what professional designers suggest:

• *Scale the bath to adult needs,* but make it accessible for the younger child. Pick standard-height counters, but add a built-in or sturdy freestanding step stool so it's easy for small fry to wash their hands and brush their teeth. Also, keep mirrors low enough for them to use. Add a lower set of towel bars and robe hooks so youngsters can pick up after themselves. In the tub, install a standard-height showerhead but include a hand-held sprayer at spout level for rinsing and cleanup.

• *Make the bath's decorative elements adaptable.* Backgrounds should be simple: easy-care, glossy paints; scrubbable vinyl-coated wall coverings; or tile. Floors should be tile with a rough, not glossy, finish for safer walking; carpet can be difficult to maintain, and hardwood floors may buckle under waves from the tub.

• *Let your child help choose the elements.* For example, team a classic striped wall covering with a wallpaper border that features the child's favorite cartoon characters or animals. The border is a small investment that you can change in a snap.

• *Pour on the color with accessories* from towels to toothbrush holders. It's especially easy to change accent colors if backdrops are kept white or neutral.

THE ESSENTIALS. For a bath that's comfortable and efficient, factor these basics into your space planning:

• **Standard tubs are 5 feet long and 30 inches wide. A comfy minimum for shower stalls is 36 inches square, although they run from 32 to 48 inches.**

• **Vanities range from 31 to 34 inches tall, but 36 inches can be easier on the back for adults.**

• **Larger sink bowls minimize splashing. Space twin sinks in the same vanity at least 12 inches apart, leaving at least 8 inches at each end of the countertop.**

• **In a shower/tub combination, mount a faucet 30 to 34 inches above the bottom of the tub. Set a shower faucet 48 to 52 inches from the bottom for ease when standing. Mount a showerhead 69 to 72 inches from the bottom.**

• **Toilet tank widths vary from about 17 to 23¼ inches. Toilets extend from the wall 25 to 30 inches. Toilet seats are usually 14 inches high.**

• **Install wall lights on either side of the vanity mirror. For shower lights in vapor-proof fixtures, locate the switch at least 6 feet away from stall.**

• **Allow at least 36 inches of towel bar space for each person using the bath. Hand towels fit on 18-inch bars; bath towels need at least 24 inches. Set towel bars 36 to 42 inches from the floor.**

• **Lower the temperature of the water heater to 105 degrees maximum to prevent burns. Also consider thermostatic faucets, which can be set to reduce scalding risks.**

PAGE 76, TOP: *Youngsters never outgrow this crisp scheme of black and white tile because it welcomes any mix of bright-hued towels and accessories. The narrow vanity maximizes space with a bump-out to accommodate the sink.*

PAGE 76, BOTTOM: *The key to this bath's success is versatility. It's personalized with the child's favorite accents—primary-color towels and tub toys. The white tile backdrop with primary accents and handsome pedestal sink are timeless*

elements. Install extra-wide, hinged vanity mirrors for concealed, convenient storage and easy grooming whether you're 6 or 16.

ABOVE: *Something's fishy in this preschooler's bath, and that makes tub time more fun. A whimsical fish border creates a chair rail effect at eye level and repeats at the ceiling. Wallpaper adds color and a backdrop that will translate to other schemes. Multicolored border tile adapts to future decorating schemes as well.*

THE TEEN YEARS

ASK YOUR TEEN WHAT HE OR SHE WANTS in a bedroom. You'll probably hear privacy first, followed by preferences for colors and phone service—and hopefully a desire for storage and study areas. This chapter addresses all those concerns, starting with tips about planning and budgeting. Although the photographs beginning on this page illustrate rooms based on specific style preferences, the colors, techniques, and projects shown easily adapt to small spruce-ups, such as fresh paint and new curtains. When possible, alternatives are given, too.

WHAT SHE WANTS

Ready to start? First, check out some art books on French painter Henri Matisse and head to the paint store. His work is so popular today that it's easy to find small books and paperbacks on his art as well as inexpensive prints and postcards. As the master of bright colors and bold combinations, Matisse created an easily imitated palette.

• *Go for color.* Choose a Matisse work you like and base your colors on his colors. Window frames, tiny built-in drawers, and abstract images—all brilliant blue—play against the apple green walls of this room.

• *Get funky.* If your daughter likes the offbeat, go for it. Matisse's famous cutout patterns translate beautifully to these closet doors. Even the floor has its own ribbon of blue-and-white cutout-like designs. (For detailed stenciling techniques, including ideas on making your own stencils, see pages 106–107.)

• *Furniture fix-ups.* A new coat of paint—and bright details—will be enough to give most pieces a new look. If your teen's room includes a chest or desk, keep on painting. (For techniques and ideas on painting furniture, see page 43 and combing on page 105.)

• *Think fresh.* Accessories make an individual statement, and best of all, great stuff can be had for little at flea markets, garage sales, and consignment shops. Look for objects—such as candlesticks or pottery—that make lamp bases or find old lamps to update with new shades. Raid your linen closet for oversize napkins that work great on small tables (see the vanity *above* and *page 78*).

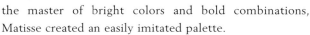

ABOVE AND RIGHT:
The colors in this room— brilliant blue, apple green, tangerine, fuchsia, and bright red—take their clues from Henri Matisse paintings and cutouts. Alternative: Art is versatile. Look through books to find a style and look that appeals to your teen. A young man might enjoy starting with nature prints, sailing scenes, or sporting themes. Base your color scheme on the browns, greens, and blues found in those types of art. (For more ideas on color selection, see page 98.)

PLANNING

A ROOM THAT GROWS UP.
Let teens express their creativity—with reasonable guidance from you. What a great opportunity for them to develop good design and budget sense while creating a place for privacy and self-expression until leaving for college. Here are some talking points:

• How much are you willing to spend? How much work do you plan to put into the project?

• How much responsibility will your teen have in terms of money, creativity, and hands-on involvement?

• What are your expectations for the project?

• Do you want the bedroom to coordinate with the flow of the house? Or is it OK to deviate from the overall style of the house? How much?

• Will posters be mounted on foam core? Or, will you allow your teen to tape them to a newly painted wall? Would a corkboard wall or a large bulletin board be an acceptable compromise?

• How does your teen express himself or herself? What is your outrageousness tolerance level?

• What colors does he or she like? Neutral, soft, or energetic palette? Do you say "no" to certain colors?

• Any preferences to patterns and fabrics? Furniture? Do you want to change or repaint?

• Which magazines, catalogs, and books will you use for ideas?

WHAT HE WANTS

Is your teen more inspired by sports and the environment than indoor decorating? If so, think eye-pleasing rather than eye-popping patterns: striped wallpaper and earth tone fabrics in tribal patterns and checks. Wood accents—bamboo-pole curtain rods, matchstick shades, and maple veneer furniture and doors—keep the mood mellow. Pair with simple and functional furniture. Visit an import store for fun and affordable accents, such as woven pillows or small rugs from India or Latin America.

MODULAR FURNITURE—IT WORKS

Today modular furniture is widely available, from chic designer to put-it-together-yourself units found at home centers and discount stores. Nothing is more functional for keeping track of huge inventories of stuff, and modular units help streamline a room. This tall bookcase and desk hutch, *page 83, top,* house loose collections of rocks, models of dinosaurs, and even pet parakeets. The no-nonsense headboard, *right,* displays books, a boom box, and clock. This vestige of Modernism should fit nicely into the 21st century.

THE CLOSET—OUT OF SIGHT, OUT OF MIND

The closet is usually the final burying ground for clutter. You can nag your teen or ignore the mess. A third alternative is to organize the closet and take off the door for maximum accessibility. Or fourth, leave the door in place but still organize with plastic-coated wire-mesh storage components. Here's how:

• ***Check out closet organizers*** at home centers and discount stores. Measure the closet and determine reasonable heights for racks and shelves, and shop accordingly. If dresses aren't a consideration, divide the entire closet into smaller compartments, *page 83, bottom.*

• ***Add a hamper with a lid to a closet or corner*** to keep dirty clothes off the floor and hidden.

• ***Consider removing sliding closet doors.*** This closet cover repeats the room's window treatments. The valance, *left,* hangs from a $1 bamboo pole by $2-a-yard leather strapping. You also can replace sliders with bifold doors, which allow easier access to the closet's contents.

LEFT: Remember bookcase headboards? They're back as efficient storage units in modular furniture. If your teen's room is starved for more storage, consider a twin bed with shelves as shown here or a full-size headboard bed. You also may be able to find a 1950s vintage headboard bed in a thrift store.

TOP RIGHT: *Open, accessible storage is the key to organization for a teen's room. It's easy to reshelve books and supplies. If you invest in a computer, get the right chair, too. (For buying tips, see pages 94–95.)*
RIGHT: *Measure the closet, discuss storage, then buy and arrange plastic-coated wire storage units to fit.*

PLANNING

FURNITURE FOR AGES AND STAGES.

• Add wall-mounted shelves or unpainted chests of drawers. Buy large containers, such as wicker baskets and aluminum wastebaskets. Let your teenager decide on color.

• Shop for a computer desk, real desk chair, and quality student desk lamp for homework. (See pages 72–73.)

• When space allows, add a comfortable lounge chair and footstool—one from a thrift store is fine as long as it's truly comfortable.

STORAGE SUGGESTIONS.

• Install Shaker pegs or hooks near the bedroom door. (See page 67 for installation tips.)

• Add extra, adjustable wall-mounted shelves. Painted or stained plywood shelves on adjustable brackets are a budget-stretching alternative to built-ins. (See page 10-11 for more about shelving.)

• Invest in a large, freestanding wardrobe—new, secondhand, or unfinished—for more storage.

• Incorporate a trunk on casters for clothes storage and a table. Stack old suitcases as a bedside or occasional table with storage.

• Place the bed against the back of a freestanding wardrobe, making a walk-in dressing area behind the bed. If a piece isn't finished on the back, staple on fabric to cover the rough edges. A matching bedsheet works well for this or try heavy-duty burlap, denim, or dark canvas. Glue or hot-glue gimp or braid over the staples for instant style.

TWIN SISTERS GROW UP

Teens yearn for separate identities, as did the twins whose rooms are featured here and on pages 86–87. Until they turned 14, the sisters shared a bedroom and used the nearby room for play and study. They declared their independence by requesting separate rooms. Here's what one of the twins and their mom did:

• *Painted the walls* with narrow yellow-and-cream stripes, softened and deepened with light yellow sponging. (For more on painting striped walls, see pages 33 and 43; for sponging techniques, see page 104.)

• *Covered the valances* for window treatments with 10-ounce canvas they painted with fabric paints.

• *Purchased a new bed,* painted pea green, as a strong design statement. One unusual and striking color sets the tone for a room. As color trends change, you can easily repaint pieces to keep up with the times.

• *Accented with pillows* in different shapes, sizes, and patterns. Note how the contemporary quilt pulls the colors together. Try a vintage quilt if you or your teen prefer a more country look.

ABOVE: *The comfy, dark, oversize chair balances the light bed, ottoman, and desk chair.*

LEFT: *An adjustable lamp illuminates texts and papers. For an accent, the mom painted a ladder-back chair in a wavy stripe motif.*

PAGE 84: *Pea green is hot; it's cool; it's here. From the furniture to the linens, this color works beautifully with blue, yellow, cream, and white.*

• *Chose a chartreuse corner nightstand* that opens cupboard-style for additional storage and bedside reading.

• *Bought a desk* with keyboard drawer to free up work space and allow the student to place her hands at the proper height when working on the computer. The recommended height for the keyboard is 26 inches from the floor to avoid straining the hands.

• *Upholstered the deep blue chair* in cozy fabric used for hiking outerwear (alternative: corduroy or soft denim).

TWIN SISTERS GROW UP

A palette of soft colors translates into a youthful but sophisticated design for the second twin sister. Here she and her mom painted blue-and-white stripes on the wall, then glazed them for softness and depth. The colors reflect the twin's distinctive taste, yet continue the general color scheme of the first bedroom. Although blue, the canvas-covered valances are made like those in the other bedroom. Other stylish ideas:

• *Use glazing to add depth* and sheen to plain walls. Dilute untinted glazing liquid from the paint store and roll over the dry walls with a small roller—known as a cigar roller. Follow the directions on the can of glazing liquid for best results. If you are unsure of the effect, test a small, hidden area before doing the entire wall.

• *Recycle old doors* into a bed. Use antique glass doorknobs for finials. Hang a narrow mirror to reflect light.

• *Shop sales and outlets* for linens and pillows to mix and match. ■**TIP** When you stay in the same color family, it's easier to mix. Repeat at least one color in every fabric you use—here blue is the choice.

• *Slipcover a chaise* in sturdy denim. Chaises can be great finds from secondhand or antiques stores. Look for 1920s to '40s pieces for good buys. Mix in striped and plaid pillows to lighten the look.

• *Invest in an antique desk*—here a pine piece—that will be a lifetime treasure. Paint an unfinished chair white for counterpoint. Or, pair a painted desk with a natural-finish chair.

This One

GROW A GARDEN ROOM

There's nothing wrong with pretty, as long as it's not sweet or cute. Actually, pretty can be cool, if you know what you're doing. It also can solve a decorating problem for you.

First, ask yourself and your daughter about the room's major problem. If it's dated, paint and fabrics in fresh, lively colors work wonders.

In this room, the existing floral-patterned wallpaper looked old and dull. Now the wallpaper peeps through new latticework like small bursts of sunshine. Most people prefer that a professional apply the lattice strips, as measuring and handling these thin pieces of wood can be a challenge. Check with a carpenter about materials, prices, and installation.

WHERE THE CEILING MEETS THE WALL, TRY EYE FOOLERY

To lower a disproportionately high ceiling, place a wallpaper border resembling hand-painted flowers below the ceiling. Carry the ceiling color onto the walls or paint the ceiling in a darker shade of the wall color.

"Raise" a low-hanging ceiling by

PAGE 88 AND ABOVE: *Refresh your daughter's room with lattice-covered walls and splashy flower motifs. Pale to summery lush colors bring this room back to life. Clean lines in the lattice and narrow windows balance stripes, flowers, solids, and unconventional patterns.*

placing a border at the top of the walls. Molding along the wall/ceiling juncture offers a similar solution. Keep the ceiling from closing in by using light colors.

GIVE THE BED ROYAL TREATMENT

A girl reigns supreme on her bed, where she holds court with her friends, talks on the phone, sprawls over homework, and lounges and daydreams. This gauzy crowning finish makes the bed a romantic focal point in flowery space.

For a similar application, you'll need about 8 to 12 yards of cotton gauze from a fabric store. The length depends on how high you hang the swag and how full you like the look.

Hang as a swag by bunching gauze around the bottom of a birdcage or other old object and securing with rubber bands. (Alternative: Use a wall-mounted drapery tieback or bracket in place of the birdcage for a sleeker look.)

Attach fabric to the lattice with wire. Cover the rubber bands and wire with decorative tassels from a fabric store.

ABOVE: *When nothing fit in this attic roost, the parents commissioned the daybed/study sofa. Subtle textures—the tapestry print and contrasting pillows on the daybed, striped chair, handcrafted iron lamp, rough-hewn coffee table, sisal rug, and campy art mural—enrich the space.*

Face it. Small, attic-type rooms are cramped. Compensate for the lack of wall—and poster—space with an eye-catching mural or fake (known to decorative painters as faux) logs. Your son won't have any more space, but he'll have a lot of fun. And if you do a ceiling mural, you'll have the beginning of a cozy study or reading retreat come empty nest time. Caution: These projects call for art skills. If decorative painting isn't your forte, begin searching for a skilled painter at your local high school, college, or university. Call instructors who teach studio art. They can recommend imaginative students who would be eager for the work as an addition to their portfolios. Moreover, a student will charge a reasonable hourly rate.

• *Interview your prospective candidates.* Review their portfolios and show them the space. Listen carefully to their feedback. Do they have fresh, original ideas that respond to your vision? Ask about the cost of materials and how long the project will take. Discuss a realistic deadline.

• *Another option:* Call the art teacher at your junior high or high school. That person may be interested in the job, especially during the summer, or may suggest a colleague.

LESSONS

• **Other sources.** Crafts shops and art supply stores often have bulletin boards studded with artists' business cards. Talk to the staff about qualified individuals.

• **For a simplified version** of the log look, see step-by-step directions on page 69.

FURNITURE AS YOU LIKE IT

Sometimes architecture boxes you in; no manufacturer on earth carries a piece for your hard-to-fit area. You're either stuck with awkward furniture placement, or you can have furniture custom made.

If you're working with designers, let them sweat the details. Discuss the purpose of the space and potential piece,

ABOVE: *Accessories lend character to any setting. Vintage pieces, such as the 1950s throw rug, guitar propped against the wall, and buffalo painting, make the room fun. Explore flea markets and secondhand stores for unusual objects.*

along with preferred styles, fabrics, and other details. Professionals will know the right people to execute the job and will guide the project to your satisfaction.

If you're on your own, do some research. Talk to friends and scout related businesses (paint stores, furniture shops, custom furnituremakers, and antiques shops) for referrals. Talk to upholsterers.

Good candidates will want input once they have inspected the space. Be prepared with photographs or sketches of what you envision. A craftsman expects your ideas, has an eye for detail, and responds with suggestions. Think twice about someone who doesn't have a lot to say.

DULLSPACE NO MORE

If your teen has a collection of mismatched furniture pieces, transform them into colorful canvases. You probably won't turn your teen loose with a spray paint can, but your artist could sketch loose and easy illustrations, then paint them. There is whimsy in exaggerated, even sloppy, figures. The budding artist can rely on color and a sense of humor.

If you and your teen need inspiration to get started, notice here how fluid, assertive strokes of paint disguise these homemade headboards. (For more on painting techniques, see pages 98–107.)

The headboards sport quirky images and messages to the pleasure of the tenants. It's argued that graffiti is art, and this artist mom's work makes the case. She and her daughters mix lively slogans with plaids, polka dots, stripes, floral prints, and happy colors. In effect, every inch of the space is their canvas. Secondhand beds work great for this treatment. If you can't find the right shape, have headboards cut from plywood and attach them to the bed frame or wall. Or, paint a headboard on the wall.

ABOVE: *Energize inexpensive directors' chairs with a little fabric paint. Even if your artistic talent amounts to little more than squiggles and lopsided polka dots, just do it. Lively color is the key. Do the same with a small table. Throw down a zippy rug and, presto, custom art! (For more on painting furniture, see page 43.)*

RIGHT: *Imagination goes a long way in revamping a homely garage apartment into fantasy quarters. So does playful sensibility and a mix of lighthearted fabrics.*

CARVE OUT WORK NICHES

Ergo-what??? The word "ergonomics" is a mouthful. And it's a lot to think about, since it means physiology, engineering, and design applied to human comfort. But in this era of technology, desk-bound students must consider comfort for their health.

• *Is the desk just for writing?* The height should measure about 30 inches.

• *Is the desk just for computer work?* The height should be about 26 inches.

• *Is there space for a key pad?*

• *Will your teen be involved in various tasks?* If so, consider multiple surface heights. Look at computer desks before you build in or adapt an old desk.

• *Can drawers and filing cabinets* be reached conveniently without strain on the back, arms, and hands? Is there adequate storage?

• *Do you want a computer chair or straight chair?* Either way, does the back of the chair support the spine? Try out several.

• *Is the chair backrest high enough* so the student can relax against it?

• *If you buy a computer chair, does the chair have a base* with five points, which could prevent tipping over?

• *Is the seat adjustable* to accommodate different tasks?

• *Does chair height adjust* so wrists rest in a natural position on the keyboard? While your teen works, the wrists should not bend forward or backward unnecessarily.

This One

PAGE 94: *When space is tight, consider turning your basement into a bedroom/study for your teen. Here the redo revolves around a platform bed with storage and a laminate desk unit. Outfit often-wasted under-the-stairs space with proper lighting and light paint. (For lighting ideas, see box at right.)*

TIP■ *Consider durable vinyl tiles as an alternative to carpet. (No more worries about pizza parties.)*

ABOVE: *A student hits the books when there's a great place to park them. Skylights and French doors light up this converted attic bedroom. Matching floral fabric and wallpaper soften the incongruous openings. Pleated shades filter harsh sunlight.*

TIP■ *Shop at stores selling used office furniture for the most chair for your money, but make sure the chair is still in good condition and offers proper support.*

WELL-LIT

LIGHTING WITH CARE. As a rule, a room needs four or five light sources, including windows. Here's a rundown of types:

• Ambient lighting bounces off walls and ceiling for background illumination. It should be evenly distributed from overhead, recessed, or track fixtures.

• Task lighting, such as a study desk lamp, provides illumination for specific jobs. Place the lamp in a corner of the desk so it casts light diagonally. The bulb should be about 15 inches above the surface and 60 to 100 watts. Use a low-brightness shade with a white lining; choose a shade broad enough to wash the work area in light.

• Your teen may prefer an easily movable multipurpose lamp. A lamp that clamps on the desk is affordable and practical.

• Light-controlling window treatments are indispensable for daytime computer use. The screen should be lit from the side rather than facing a window.

• Lighting for bedside should be in the 60- to 100-watt range for incandescent bulbs. The standard bedside lamp height is 28 to 32 inches. Use an opaque shade so the light will shine upward and downward. Swing-arm lamps with three-way bulbs work well for reading in bed, as the light can be easily adjusted.

• Depending on furniture arrangement and space, a floor lamp or extra table lamp is ideal for an additional reading area. For reading in a chair, light should be coming over your shoulder; 75 to 100 watts is recommended for most readers.

MAKING YOUR MARK

INSPIRED BY ROOMS OR IDEAS IN CHAPTERS One through Four? Ready to brush up on your painting and wallpapering skills or learn some new ones? This chapter includes the basics, plus specialty techniques for walls and floors. If you like the murals featured throughout the book, see the simplified how-to directions on pages 102–103. To make it easy, we list recommended supplies for each technique or project.

PAINT PRIMER

Have you noticed how color sets the themes for the rooms in chapters One through Four? That's no accident, because color is the most important decorating tool and paint is the cheapest.

There are no longer strict rules about what color goes with what color. Children's rooms are no longer restricted to primary colors; in fact, happy mixes of bright primary, secondary, and tertiary colors are all the rage. Likewise, nurseries now go beyond strictly pastels. What is important in mixing is to choose colors with the same degree of intensity. If you use a bright, clear, fire engine red in a room, make sure a pink and green you use are equally vibrant. ■**TIP** For a no-fail scheme, start with your favorite color and turn to the color wheel to choose adjacent colors as your accents.

COLOR WHEEL BASICS

To understand how color works, start with the basics.
- *Primary colors*—red, yellow, and blue—are the colors from which all others originate.
- *Secondary colors* are mixed from primaries and are orange (red and yellow), green (yellow and blue), and violet (blue and red).
- *Tertiary colors* are primary colors combined with their nearest secondary color and include blue-green, yellow-green, yellow-orange, red-orange, and blue-purple.
- *Complementary colors* are opposite or near-opposite color combinations: red and green, yellow and violet, orange and blue.
- *Tints are colors mixed with white,* such as pink, which is derived from red and white. Shades are black added to a color, such as navy, maroon, midnight blue, and deep purple.

COLOR CLUES

When you go to the paint store, take bright toys, a fabric sample, wallpaper, or anything you'd like to match for color. Take home three to five samples of paint chips in your color range. Vertically tack up the paint chips in your child's room. Observe the colors at different times of day and with artificial and natural light. Narrow your choices to two or three colors. Buy a pint of each and paint a small wallboard scrap or wall section in your choices. Live with these a day or two before you decide. Remember that the larger the painted areas, the stronger the color will appear. If the color you choose seems to be overpowering, switch to a lighter value of the paint chip.

THE RIGHT MATERIALS

Before you can do any of the specialty finishes on pages 100–107, you have to have a clean, blank surface. So whether you're planning to try your hand at the apple tree mural on page 103 or the freehand door art on page 101, or you're just perking up your child's room with fresh paint, start with this basic supply list:

- Primer
- Paint (see box at right to calculate the amount you need)
- Brown paper drop cloths for the floor; heavy plastic drop cloths for furniture
- Surfacing compound and knife to apply it, sandpaper, painter's tape, edger
- Metal paint pan, plastic liners, roller with threaded handle for extensions, sash, and trim brushes. Most interior jobs call for a 7- or 9-inch roller frame. Use a long pole for the ceiling and short pole (2 feet long) for walls.

PAINTS WITH A PURPOSE

Paint makes it a snap to give a baby's or child's room personal style. New easy-to-use specialty paints—chalkboard, glitter, and glow-in-the-dark—and colors formulated in crayon hues simplify decorating. A child's fondness for drawing translates into a blackboard painted on the wall, *left*. The chalkboard paint applies to almost any wall or floor surface without special priming. Here's how to paint your own:

- *Calculate how high* to paint the board. Measure your child's reach; add 3 or 4 inches for growth.
- *Use a steel measuring tape*, level, and hard pencil to position and draw the board on the wall.
- *Outline the chalkboard with painter's tape* (not masking tape, as it can remove the paint when pulled off). Apply a second band of tape 2 to 4 inches around the outside to create a border. Paint inside the border with chalkboard paint; follow manufacturer's directions for best results.
- *Brighten the border* with rubber-stamp designs.

ABOVE RIGHT: *Give your child drawing room with a blackboard painted directly on the wall. Specialty paint from the paint store makes it easier.*

ABOVE LEFT: *For extra fun, combine easy sponged ceiling clouds with stenciled and hand-painted designs.*

PLANNING

CALCULATING COVERAGE.

Paint cans usually state the one-coat coverage you can expect from 1 gallon of paint or primer. For many paints, including primers, a gallon will cover about 400 square feet. But it's still a good idea to calculate coverage. Measure the perimeter of the room (all walls). Multiply the result by the ceiling height to get the square footage. Round off to the full foot. Don't deduct for windows or other openings unless they add up to more than 100 square feet (unlikely for a child's bedroom). Divide that figure into the number of square feet that a gallon of paint promises to cover. Round up to the nearest whole number and buy as accurately as possible, as it is difficult to match paint if you need more or dispose of properly if you buy too much.

TIPS/SAFETY. Because of the time and labor involved, it pays to purchase quality paint, brushes, and rollers. You'll find a top-quality paint rolls on smoothly and evenly and will have the depth of color lacking in some bargain paints. For children's rooms, use semigloss latex paint, which is easier to wash than a flat finish.

Lead paint, often found in older houses, has been linked to learning problems in children. If you are redoing an older house, don't let young children play in areas with paint chips. Pregnant women also should not chip or strip suspected lead paint.

This one

PAINT LIKE A PRO

Whether you are painting floors, as shown *near right*; doors, *page 101*; or simply giving walls a fresh coat of paint, technique counts. Use these two pages for basic techniques to get started.

FLOORS

Paint provides a fun alternative to wall-to-wall carpet. Although you probably wouldn't paint beautiful hardwoods that are in excellent condition, why not be creative by painting worn hardwoods or a particleboard subfloor? Here's how to do it:

• *Measure your room.*

• *Transfer measurements* to graph paper and chart out a check repeat that minimizes partial checks around the edges. (This floor uses 18-inch squares.)

• *To prepare a wood floor for painting,* fill gaps with wood filler and sand smooth. To make the job easier, you'll probably want to rent a small hand sander designed for do-it-yourself projects. Don't use a large commercial sander designed for refinishing.

• *Pick up sanding residue* with a tack rag.

• *Paint the entire floor* in the lighter shade.

• *Let dry.*

• *Sand slightly.* Pick up sanding residue again with a tack rag.

• *Mark your pattern* only along the floor edges, using a straightedge and gray charcoal pencil.

• *Stretch a chalk line* across the room between markings; snap lines to create the pattern.

• *Tape off darker squares* using 1½-inch-wide, quick-release masking tape.

• *Rub the edges to secure* the tape to the floor.

• *For a clean edge,* spread a light coat of acrylic matte medium (available at art supply stores) along the edge of the masking tape. This product dries clear and secures the edges.

• *Paint the squares* with two coats of the darker color (red here) of your choice.

• *Allow adequate drying time* between coats.

• *For a long-lasting painted finish,* seal the floor with two or more coats of matte-finish, nonyellowing polyurethane.

WALL PREPARATION DOES PAY

Before you paint any wall, scrape or sand away rough spots. (If necessary, strip old wallpaper. A spray-on liquid stripper combined with scoring the walls is less cumbersome than renting a

ABOVE: *Check with your paint store for the best paint for the type and condition of your existing wood floor. Oil-based enamels are durable for high-traffic areas. Colors are more limited, but there are also paints formulated for floors and porches.*

steamer. If you do have to rent a steamer to remove stubborn paper, follow the directions carefully. If any glossy surfaces remain, dull them with sandpaper or liquid sandpaper.) Scrub walls with mild detergent and water. Rinse with a sponge and clear water. For mold and mildew, wash with a solution of 1 quart of household bleach and 3 quarts of water.

PAINT PRELIMINARIES

• *Always prime.* (Treat stained spots with a special primer that prevents bleed-through.) Don't paint over wet walls or the paint won't hold.

• *If the weather dampens* the walls inside or out, run an air-conditioner or dehumidifier or wait for more favorable conditions.

FINALLY, LET'S DO IT

Precondition a synthetic roller cover by rinsing it with water and spinning dry. (Do not precondition a lamb's-wool roller.) Use a metal tray, with disposable plastic tray liners, as it's more stable than a paint can and can be attached to a ladder. Fill only one-third of the tray with paint. Load the roller by rolling it in the deeper end of the tray, then smoothing it on the sloping surface until the paint is distributed evenly. Paint the ceiling first, starting with a narrow strip at the ceiling line, then walls around openings and along the baseboards. Use a brush, edging roller, or paint pad for this; use a small brush or trim roller for corners.

• *When applying paint* to large surfaces, make a letter M (3 feet across and 3 feet high); then fill in spaces, working from the unpainted area into the wet paint.

If you are using the same paint for walls and woodwork, paint the woodwork as you get to it. If the woodwork will be another color, paint it after you have completed the walls.

• *Paint doors in this order:* door frame, top, back, and front edges. Paint a paneled door in this order: panels and molding, the rest of the door (starting at the top). Paint around hardware you can't remove, using a trim brush. Fill in carefully with a small trim brush. Protect the floor or carpet with masking tape or with a cardboard or plastic guard.

ABOVE: *Run out of surfaces to paint in your child's room? Frame a youthful design and start painting the door. See the box at right for how-to-do-it details.*

COLOR CUES

SPECIALTY DOOR PAINTING TECHNIQUES. A whimsical painting like the one at *left* doesn't require special art skills. Go with bright colors and basic shapes. This is also a good parent-child project, as the canvas is only a door and the required materials are limited. Handprints also could be a fun project for preschoolers.

• Lightly sketch the design with a hard art pencil (at least a #5 or #6). Use acrylic paints and seal with a finishing coat of clear polyurethane, which makes the door easy to wipe clean.

For extra punch, repeat the colors in your art for other door frames and window frames in the room. As an alternative, stencil all or part of your door creation. Experiment first on paper to make sure you and your child like the look. For more on stenciling techniques, see pages 106–107.

DECOUPAGE ALTERNATIVE. Select paper art such as wallpaper cutouts or motifs from heavy gift wrap. Or, experiment with clip art you tint with colored pencils, see page 22.

Decide how to place cutouts on a clean, painted door.

Use decoupaging liquid (a clear crafts glue) to adhere the cutouts and seal them to the surface. To seal, brush over two to three coats of the liquid. Allow the surface to dry completely between coats. For how-to techniques, see page 61.

MURAL, MURAL ON YOUR WALL

In the mood for a creative project with room-changing results? Here are two different techniques you can use. Try one or both for the look you want. The easiest is one that uses an overhead projector, such as was used for this friendly apple tree, *page 103*. Its spreading limbs and shiny red apples, beneath soft clouds and a periwinkle sky, brighten the room. The projector technique will work with any simple motif. The other technique is to draw a mural freehand.

WHERE TO FIND THE IMAGE

Look for an image that has strong lines and is easily traceable. In the case of the apple tree, apples on a rug inspired a mother.

This freehand wall painting, *right*, is stylized, not truly dimensional, so don't sweat the details of every little twig and knothole. Line and color, somewhat exaggerated, create charm, as does the off-center positioning of the image on two adjacent walls.

MURAL MAGIC

Sketch paper and pencil
#5 or #6 hard pencil
Scrap of plywood or poster board (optional)
Acrylic paints in three shades each of brown and green
*   and one shade of pale yellow*
Paintbrushes
Three natural sponges

1. Sketch some designs on paper before you draw on the wall, using the tree motif, *above*, for inspiration. Keep the sketch simple, focusing on the main features: the trunk, branches, and large blocks of leaves.

2. Using #5 or #6 pencil, lightly sketch the design on the wall. See Step 5 of Apple Tree Mural, page 103, for instructions.

3. If you haven't painted with acrylics before, practice on a scrap of plywood or poster cardboard to perfect your tech-

ABOVE: *Although the artist used varying shades of green and brown for this tree mural, you can paint a charming folk art version with one brown paint and one green and no shading or highlights.*

nique. Work with watered-down acrylics and paint a small section of the trunk, branch, and leaves at one time, as directed below.

4. Water down the darkest shade of brown paint to the consistency of wall paint. Paint the darkest areas of the trunk and branches first, referring to Step 8 of the Apple Tree Mural for instructions and suggestions. Apply at least two more shades of brown, each lighter than the preceding one, to suggest perspective and roundness. For the leaves, use dampened natural sponges to dab on three shades of green. Sponge the wall with the darkest shade first and finish with the lightest on top. Don't let the paint dry between colors; blend paint between colors for a subtle, natural appearance. Add highlights by sponging on and blending in dabs of pale yellow.

LEFT: *Repeat the dominant color from the mural—here apple red—for key accents in the scheme. Note the red drawer pulls on the white chest. Red apples also dot the cotton rug (out of view).*

APPLE TREE MURAL

Periwinkle blue flat latex wall paint for ceiling

Roller brush or wide paintbrush; paint pan

White spray paint (about 10 cans for a moderate-size room)

Flat latex interior wall paint (in your desired color) as background on the walls

Tracing paper

Overhead projector (you can rent one from a rental or school supply store)

#5 or #6 hard pencil (available at art supply stores)

Precut apple and leaf stencils or materials for cutting your own stencils (see page 107)

Stencil crayons (available at art supply stores) for a dimensional effect or flat latex interior paints for a solid, coloring book effect

Stencil brushes or paintbrushes

Heavy paper

1. Protect the floor with drop cloths. Make sure the room is well ventilated and the windows are open. Paint the ceiling blue; let dry. Wearing protective clothing, glasses, and a mask, spray-paint hazy white clouds on the ceiling. Be sure to keep the room well ventilated, but close the door so white paint doesn't blow into any other room.

2. Paint the room's walls in your color choice; let dry.

3. Locate an image of a tree with out-spread limbs. Trace the image onto tracing paper. Using an overhead projector, project the tracing-paper image as large as you wish on the wall. This image was enlarged to run over onto an adjacent wall.

4. Determine the size of the apple and leaf motifs and cut out stencils. You'll need one stencil for the apple and one stencil each for the three sizes of leaves. ■**TIP** For the strongest impact, the size of the apples and leaves should be slightly exaggerated on the tree. If you are using precut stencils, hold them up to the projected image and adjust the tree shape accordingly. Set stencils aside.

5. Lightly draw the projected tree image on the wall using hard pencil. Don't press down, or it will leave hard-to-remove marks. Also, do not erase; an eraser leaves greaselike marks that will show. If you project the image on two walls, be aware that the image will distort somewhat. Compensate by lengthening and shortening as needed when tracing the image on the wall.

6. Lightly draw the stencil motifs on the tree as directed in Step 5, overlapping the leaves and apples for a more realistic look.

7. To use the stencil crayons, first stroke the crayon on heavy paper, then dab the stroked area with a clean, dry stencil brush. Hold the stencil to the wall; then, using a straight up-and-down motion of the brush, dab the color inside the stencil. Never color the wall directly with the crayon.

8. To create perspective with the stencil crayons, first determine where light will strike the image, then color the shapes beginning with the darkest shades and moving to the lightest. For our apple tree, the right side of the trunk was heavily shaded, with white highlights sweeping down the trunk just left of center. The round shape is further suggested with narrow but heavy shading on the left side of the trunk. To "ground" the tree, create dark shading where roots spread. Also add dark shading at crevices where the limbs begin and spread. To give dimension to the apples, use dark shading at the outer edges; then add white highlights to create a play of sunlight and to emphasize the dips for the stems. Shade the leaves darker at the outer edges but create larger areas of highlighting on leaves in the center of the tree and smaller areas of highlighting on leaves around the outside.

9. If you prefer a coloring book effect, simply fill in the shapes with solid colors of latex paint.

Decorative Painting: Just the Facts

SPONGING

If you want a lively statement of texture and color without hassles, try sponging. All it takes is a little dipping and patting for an incredible finish. Here's how:

- *If you are working* on a previously unpainted surface, apply primer coat or an extra coat of base paint to the walls for a smooth finish.
- *Paint a solid base coat* of your choice color and let it dry overnight. Don't rush the drying.
- *Test your technique* and color combination in a hidden place on a wall or on scrap board.
- *Wear disposable plastic gloves* instead of household rubber gloves, which leave fingerprint impressions. Change gloves as needed.
- *Use a natural sea sponge* instead of a synthetic one to achieve a soft, mottled appearance. Vary the sizes for interesting effects.
- *To begin, wet your sponge* with water, wringing it out thoroughly. This makes the paint adhere better to the sponge.
- *Pour a small amount of paint* into an old plate or pie tin and dip the sponge into it.
- *Cover the sponge* with a small amount of paint—too much will weigh it down. Use a newspaper to blot excess.
- *Cup the sponge in your hand* and push lightly onto the surface. Practice first.
- *Space the patches of color evenly,* but change the position of the sponge for an irregular, mottled effect. Close, overlapping marks have a sleek look; widely spaced sponging with little or no overlap produces a casual appearance. Try spaced first, then fill in.
- *To apply several layers of color,* dab the first color over the surface. Let it dry. Apply the second and third layers the same way.

RAG ROLLING

For a textured finish, use this technique. The look varies with the rag fabric you use. As with other techniques, practice. Here's how:

- *Rag rolling requires completing* a whole wall or a room at one time for best effect.
- *Two people are usually needed*: one to apply the glaze, the other to follow with the rag. You need to be able to work quickly.
- *Use any type of cloth*—cotton sheets, burlap, cloth diapers, or cheesecloth. Prepare fabric by twisting it into tight, 6-inch-long sausagelike rolls. Prepare enough rolls to do an entire wall or room. A 12×14-foot room may

ABOVE: *Sponging creates an ideal background for other wall treatments and can be used as part of a mural.*

PAGE 105, TOP: *Rag rolling textures a wall but creates a finish that's easy to paint over.*

PAGE 105, BOTTOM: *Combing is most fun when lines aren't perfectly straight. Try it on furniture, too.*

need as much as the equivalent of a double-bed sheet. Make sure you have enough rolls.

• *Use glossy or semigloss paint* because it won't be absorbed easily by the wall or rag.

• *Apply a base coat* of semigloss paint or thinned glaze; let it dry completely.

• *Apply a second coat* of a different complementary color, using a roller or brush. ■**TIP** Make sure the background color is several shades lighter than the paint you apply on top. Otherwise you can't see it.

• *While the second coat is still wet,* roll the rag roll lightly over the surface from top to bottom, holding it at both ends. This action partially removes the new top color, exposing the base coat. If you haven't ragged, practice first.

• *Change direction often.* Discard the fabric roll once it becomes saturated.

COMBING

This technique is as fun for furniture as it is for walls—and much easier. For furniture, seal the final dry top coat with clear, matte-finish polyurethane. Here are combing basics:

• *Apply a base coat,* using any type of paint. ■**TIP** Semigloss and high-gloss paints make a slick surface for combing; flat is usually easier to work with. Let dry completely.

• *Apply a complementary color* of paint over the first layer. The top layer will darken the color of the undercoat somewhat.

• *Comb the surface* while the new layer is still wet, using a comb or other toothed instrument. A piece of heavy cardboard works, too.

• *Begin at the top of the wall*—in a corner—and pull the comb through the paint or glaze. An extra hand is helpful for this step. While you brush on the coating, your partner follows and combs through the paint before it dries. (For a small piece of furniture, such as a chest, you probably won't need help.)

• *Use long, clean strokes* and wipe the comb clean after each run across or down the wall.

• *Comb in the direction you prefer.* The design does not require totally straight lines. Comb squiggly horizontal lines or bold vertical stripes if you like them.

DECORATIVE PAINTING WITH

Because stenciling has its own vocabulary, tools, and techniques, it may seem complicated at first. But it's only as complicated as you make it. Start simple and see how it goes. Each type of paint and method of application creates a different effect, and experimentation is fun. Practice first on scraps of plywood or cardboard; then go ahead and play. Arts and crafts stores carry a variety of supplies. If you haven't stenciled before, purchase small quantities of several types of paints, brushes, and stencils and experiment to find the ones that work best for you.

MATERIALS YOU'LL NEED

• *Stencil brushes,* except for smaller brushes used for detail work, are generally packed with blunt-cut bristles. Artists prefer natural bristles because of their smooth finish, easy cleanup, and long life. Buy sizes according to your project.

• *Overlays,* which are thin sheets of plastic with cutouts, make creating a stencil possible in several steps (the number is indicated on the packaging). For example, the first overlay of a floral design may contain only the leaves; the second may cover the leaves but contain petal cutouts. Keep in mind that overlays may not match the number of colors used in the pattern. Some designs call for multiple colors in one overlay. Also, the number of overlays does not determine the complexity of the stencil. (For example, a stencil with three overlays can require the same amount of surface area as a stencil with nine or more overlays.)

• *Bridges* are small areas of uncut plastic integrated into the design to keep the stencil from falling apart. They contribute significantly to the design but may not be found in some stencils. Check packages and directions to be sure.

• *Registration marks,* cutouts, and markings on each overlay serve as guides to keep the design straight and each overlay in position. You'll need these for a neat job.

• *Stencil cards* are the old-fashioned form of stencils (most stencils today are cut from a film of clear polyester or acetate). Similar in thickness to a manila folder, they are good for single-element stenciling with few repeats.

PAINT CHOICES

• *Liquid acrylics* come in bright colors in lots of shades that blend easily to make lighter or darker hues. They dry quickly and clean up easily with water, but you'll have little time for mixing and shading. They give soft, thin coloration when you dab some paint off the brush before applying it to your surface, and they are good for detailed projects.

• *Paint creams,* relatively new on the market, produce more intense colors than liquids when more pigment is picked up on the brush. They are the consistency of shoe polish so they won't run or spill. Use creams when you want a blendable, powdery finish, as they can be brushed from the jar to the wall. Try the newer bright shades.

STENCILS

cils in place on the wall so you don't have to hold them by hand. It leaves no sticky residue. Stencil adhesive works, too, but can leave stencils tacky.

DO-IT-YOURSELF STENCILS

- *Paint sticks,* actually solid tubes, are easy to use for stencilers of all levels. Paint sticks are available at fine art stores and through mail-order stencil catalogs. Use by dabbing them with a brush then dabbing on the design.
- *Paint crayons* are rubbed on a plastic plate before you use them on your surface. This allows you to control shading.
- *Extenders,* liquids added to acrylic paints to keep them from drying too fast, allow time for shading and blending.

TECHNIQUES

- *Dry-brush application,* a standard technique used to apply paint, requires minimal paint on the brush. Dabbing on a paper towel to remove excess paint is common.
- *Stippling* applies stencil paint in an up-and-down motion and creates a fine, textural effect (depending on the amount of paint on the brush). This often-used method allows you to lightly apply the paint and keeps the pigment from brushing or seeping under cutout designs.
- *Swirling* gives a smooth rather than powdery finish by applying a small amount of paint in a downward, twisting motion. It results in dark or light effects, depending on the amount of pressure you exert.
- *Painter's tape* applied around the stencil edges keeps sten-

- *You'll need clear acetate sheets* (available at crafts stores), paper, masking tape, pencil, fine-point marker, stencil brushes, and a crafts knife.
- *Draw your stencil pattern on paper.*
- *Plan colors and number of stencils you need.* Use more than one stencil when the pattern is detailed; if patterns overlap, use one stencil for each color.
- *Tape an acetate sheet over your pattern* and trace, with a fine-point marker, the area to be cut away.
- *If the design requires a second stencil,* outline the pattern you cut away in the previous stencil on this stencil. The outlines serve as guides for aligning successive stencils. Use a crafts knife to cut the stencils to the exact shapes and sizes you need for your design.
- *To paint,* first tape the pattern in place.
- *Dip tip of stencil brush* into the paint, dabbing off excess on newsprint or on a clean cotton rag.
- *Dab on paint to fill the cutout area,* moving from the edges inward. The paint should leave a powdery finish.
- *When using more than one stencil,* carefully remove the first one and let the paint dry. Align the guides on the second one, tape it in place, and paint.

WALLPAPER BASICS

Y ou may have noticed this rather odd fact about wallpaper: It's priced by the roll, but is usually packaged by the continuous double or triple roll bolt. An American single roll is 36 square feet. (If you happen to use English- or French-made paper, it's 29 square feet.) Even though it's tempting to order just enough, order extra. It's tricky to get dye-lots to match, and you want perfect matches. To match patterns, figure 36 square feet will give you 30 square feet to use. If you have calculated and ordered wallpaper before, you may feel comfortable using a store's estimating chart. But it never hurts to carefully measure a room (see page 99 for measuring tips) and to ask for help at a wallpaper store for confidence in the amount you purchase.

• *Start fresh.* Remove old wallpaper. Try to pull up a corner; if it's strippable, it peels easily. If it isn't, be prepared to work hard. First try a spray-on liquid wallpaper stripper. Follow the bottle directions for scoring (slashing with a sharp knife) and soaking. If a spray works, your job isn't so bad. If it doesn't, rent a professional steamer or buy a small one. The small steamer takes longer, but it's easier and safer to handle. As with the spray, it's important to score the wallpaper to soften the paste. To finish the job, you'll need a 6-inch-wide putty (broad) knife for scraping and more liquid wallpaper stripper to remove paste residue. Always allow a stripped wall to dry at least 24 hours.

No time to hand-paint or stencil a room? Wallpaper for an instant new look and color scheme. For a teenage girl's room, a floral paper with matching fabric creates a flower garden retreat from what had been a tucked-away space.

• *Technique.* If the wall to be papered has been painted, preparation may not be too trying. Simply patch hairline cracks and nail holes with surfacing compound, sand the walls, and prime them with wallpaper primer-sealer. Make sure you buy a primer for wallpaper; don't be tempted to use leftover paint primer. If you removed old wallpaper, you also will need to prime with the wallpaper primer-sealer. Check at the paint store to make sure you are buying the correct primer. When it's finally time to hang paper, enlist some help. It's easier as a two-person job. And if you haven't hung paper before, or not in a long time, it's a good idea to check out a video from your public library for a demonstration.

A LAST RESORT

What if old wallpaper won't budge? Do you have to steam it off? If it's well attached except for a few places that you can easily glue down, you can paint over it. Here's how:

• *Wash the walls* with a solution of trisodium phosphate (TSP) or residue-free cleaner to remove dirt and grease.

• *Glue down all seams* and loose areas that catch paint.

• *Apply a sealing primer* to old or inexpensive paper wall

• **Hang the first strip with absolute care.** It must be truly vertical for proper alignment. Use a plumb bob (a small tool with a pull-out string coated with chalk) or a level. Measure the width of the wall covering from your starting point. Subtract ½ inch and mark your plumb line. Hang the first strip to the left of this line. Cut the first two strips so the patterns match; they should be several inches longer than the wall height. You can trim for perfect fit.

• **If you are using prepasted strips,** reroll the patterned side in, starting from the bottom. Place the roll in a water box so the top of the strip comes out of the box. Place the box on the floor below where the strip will be hung. Draw the roll up onto the wall and smooth into position along the plumb line.

• **Smooth with a wall brush** or clean sponge to eliminate air pockets. Double-check the position; trim excess with a sharp utility knife and a straightedge.

• **Carefully line up the second strip to the first.** Wait 15 minutes and smooth butted edges with a seam roller. Remove squeezed-out paste with a sponge and clean water.

• **To apply unpasted wallpaper,** use the adhesive recommended by the manufacturer. If you have questions, ask at the wallpaper store or home center. Place the first strip on a pasting table, face down; spread paste on it from the center to the top edge. Fold the top half of the strip back to the center, pasted surfaces together. Be careful not to crease. Repeat with bottom half following same technique.

• **If you cut all strips at once for a room,** mark the correct end up and number the strips. Hang the first strip by opening the top half and lining up the motif at the top. Smooth to the wall, unfold, and smooth the bottom half.

• **Deal with openings as you come to them.** Let the strip that is adjoining the opening overlap the casings. Crease at the vertical edge and cut with a razor blade or extra-sharp knife. Be extremely careful; it's easy to slice a finger. Then crease and cut at the top of the casing and for windows underneath.

■**TIP** *Here's how to deal with corners.* Measure from the edge of your last strip to the corner. Cut a piece ½ inch wider. Hang it, bending the ½-inch margin around the corner. Snap a plumb line on the second wall. Use this as a guide and hang the next strip so it overlaps the ½-inch margin and extends ½ inch back around the corner. Cut through both thicknesses. Peel off the top strip, lift the edge, and peel the inner layer. Roll the exposed seams.

coverings because they will soak up the water in latex paint and possibly loosen any wallpaper underneath.

• **Rough a vinyl or vinyl-coated paper** with steel wool or sandpaper. Use primer for shiny surfaces before applying latex paint.

• **Mask apparent imperfections** with a faux finish, such as sponging, glazing, and ragging. For ideas, see pages 104–105.

STARTING WITH THE BASICS

• **Plan the match.** You will have to trim the last strip you put up to meet the first strip. To minimize the problem, begin where this won't be obvious, such as at a door or window.

BORDERS & CEILINGS

Borders work wonders—at chair-rail or ceiling height or around a window. But don't cut a wall in half with a border; your child's room will literally look chopped in two. Unless you are only doing a small area—around a window or mirror in a bath—this is a job for two people. Follow these tips, and your borders will pass inspection.

• *Let a wall covering dry* 48 hours before mounting a border on top of it. If you don't, the layers may not dry well.

• *When hanging a prepasted border* over a wall covering, do not wet the border, as it may not adhere properly. Instead, use an adhesive designed for use over wall coverings, such as vinyl-over-vinyl adhesive. If in doubt, ask at the wallpaper store.

• *When hanging a prepasted border* on a painted wall, prime the wall in the border area with a primer designed to help the adhesive stick. (See page 108 for information about primers.)

• *Don't just wet and apply* a prepasted border to a painted wall. The borders must sit for a few minutes before hanging. To activate the adhesive, soak the borders for the amount of time indicated in the directions.

• *To simplify handling,* fold a wet prepasted border accordion style (without·creasing); make sure the adhesive side never touches the front. Your partner should hold the folded end while you position small sections on the wall.

• *After positioning the border,* use a sponge to smooth out wrinkles and help the border adhere properly.

SAY "YES" TO CEILINGS

Take good design to new heights. Wallpaper the ceiling and give your kids something to gaze at when they're lying around.

BELOW LEFT: *Grab your child's attention at eye level. Place a border in line with the windowsill to avoid chopping up the room with a second horizontal line. Two wallpapers, above and below the border, attract everyone's attention. Playful primary colors and shapes create interest and whimsy without being too busy.*

This job takes two people. (For examples of this lighthearted, papered-ceiling look, see pages 50–51.)

• **Essential tool.** A wooden T-bar made from 2×4s helps hold the paper to the ceiling while it's smoothed into place. Cut the top crosspiece about 3 feet long; cut the leg piece about 4 feet long. Screw the pieces together.

• **Measure accurately.** Measure the width of the wall covering and subtract ½ inch from that measurement. Mark this dimension at each end of the ceiling. Snap a chalk line connecting these two points, using a plumb bob (a small tool with a pull-out string coated with chalk). This line will be your straight guide and help you paper neatly.

• **Cut and paste.** Cut the wallpaper for the first strip; allow a 2-inch overlap on each end. If you're hanging prepasted wall covering, roll it loosely and dip it in warm water. Let the paper rest 15 minutes. For paper that is not prepasted, apply adhesive to half the strip, leaving 1 inch unpasted at the top to hold on to. Fold it over, then paste the other half, and fold it over. Let the paper rest 15 minutes. Before applying the paper, roll the paste over the ceiling with a short-napped roller. Align one end of the paper at the edge of the ceiling.

• **To keep the paper in place,** have your partner anchor it by pressing the T-bar against the end. Carefully unroll or unfold the wallpaper and smooth it into place with a brush. (Keep the paper aligned with the chalk line.) Have your partner move the T-bar across the ceiling as you work.

• **Trim the excess paper** with a crafts knife and metal ruler. Push ruler edge into the ceiling and wall seam to crease, then trim along the line. Remove excess paste with a damp sponge.

TOO MUCH CEILING? TRIM IT INSTEAD

Paste the border around the perimeter of the ceiling (abutting the seam where the wall and ceiling meet). Or, come in toward the center, leaving several inches of open space between the seam and border. Embellish the center or corners of the ceiling. Borders that take the corner at an angle soften the edges of a room. (For example, cut scallop motifs from extra border paper and paste at an angle to create a fan shape in the corners of the ceiling.)

BELOW CENTER: *Trick the eye comfortably by dropping the border to meet the top of the window and door and to emphasize an existing horizontal line. The striped paper pulls the eye upward, adding visual height to make a cramped room appear larger.*

BELOW RIGHT: *A wallpaper border gives this room character. Frame windows and doors with a border that can be read both vertically and horizontally. You already have straight lines around the windows and doors as your guides.*

INDEX

Numbers in **bold** indicate pages with project instructions.

U.S. UNITS TO METRIC EQUIVALENTS

To Convert From	Multiply By	To Get
Inches	25.4	Millimeters (mm)
Inches	2.54	Centimeters (cm)
Feet	30.48	Centimeters (cm)
Feet	0.3048	Meters (m)

METRIC UNITS TO U.S. EQUIVALENTS

To Convert From	Multiply By	To Get
Millimeters	0.0394	Inches
Centimeters	0.3937	Inches
Centimeters	0.0328	Feet
Meters	3.2808	Feet